GENESIS to REVELATION

A Comprehensive Verse-by-Verse Exploration of the Bible

MINOR PROPHETS

GENE M. TUCKER

LEADER GUIDE

GENESIS to REVELATION

A Comprehensive Verse-by-Verse Exploration of the Bible

MINOR PROPHETS

GENE M. TUCKER

LEADER GUIDE

GENESIS TO REVELATION SERIES: **MINOR PROPHETS**

LEADER GUIDE

ISBN 9781501855849

Manufactured in the United States of America

19 20 21 22 23 24 25 26 27 28 — 10 9 8 7 6 5 4 3 2 1

ABINGDON PRESS
Nashville

HOW TO TEACH GENESIS TO REVELATION

Unique Features of This Bible Study

In Genesis to Revelation, you and your class will study the Bible in three steps. Each step provides a different level of understanding of the Scripture. We call these steps Dimension One, Dimension Two, and Dimension Three.

Dimension One concerns what the Bible actually says. You do not interpret the Scripture at this point; you merely take account of what it says. Your main goal for this dimension is to get the content of the passage clear in your mind. What does the Bible say?

Dimension One is in workbook form. The members of the class will write the answers to questions about the passage in the space provided in the participant book. All the questions in Dimension One can be answered by reading the Bible itself. Be sure the class finishes Dimension One before going on to Dimensions Two and Three.

Dimension Two concerns information that will shed light on the Scripture under consideration. Dimension Two will answer such questions as

- What are the original meanings of some of the words used in the passage?

- What is the original background of the passage?

- Why was the passage most likely written?

- What are the relationships between the persons mentioned in the passage?

- What geographical and cultural factors affect the meaning of the passage?

The question for Dimension Two is, What information do we need in order to understand the meaning of the passage? In Dimension One the class members will discover what the Bible says. In Dimension Two they will discover what the Bible means.

Dimension Three focuses on interpreting the Scripture and applying it to life situations. The questions here are

- What is the meaning of the passage for my life?

- What response does the passage require of me as a Christian?

- What response does this passage require of us as a group?

Dimension Three questions have no easy answers. The task of applying the Scripture to life situations is up to you and the class.

Aside from the three-dimensional approach, another unique feature of this study is the organization of the series as a whole. Classes that choose to study the Genesis to Revelation Series will be able to study all the books of the Bible in their biblical order. This method will give the class continuity that is not present in most other Bible studies. The class will read and study virtually every verse of the Bible, from Genesis straight through to Revelation.

Weekly Preparation

Begin planning for each session early in the week. Read the passage that the lesson covers, and write the answers to Dimension One questions in the participant book. Then read Dimensions Two and Three in the participant book. Make a note of any questions or comments you have. Finally, study the material in the leader guide carefully. Decide how you want to organize your class session.

Organizing the Class Session

Since Genesis to Revelation involves three steps in studying the Scripture, you will want to organize your class sessions around these three dimensions. Each lesson in the participant book and this leader guide consists of three parts.

The first part of each lesson in the leader guide is the same as the Dimension One section in the participant book, except that the leader guide includes the answers to Dimension One questions. These questions and answers are taken from the New International Version of the Bible.

You might use Dimension One in several ways:

1. Ask the group members to read the Scripture and to write the answers to all the Dimension One questions before coming to class. This method will require that the class covenant to spend the necessary amount of study time outside of class. When the class session begins, read through the Dimension One questions, asking for responses from the group members. If anyone needs help with any of the answers, look at the biblical reference together.

2. Or, if you have enough class time, you might spend the first part of the session working through the Dimension One questions together as a group. Locate the Scripture references, ask the questions one at a time, and invite the class members to find the answers and to read them aloud. Then allow enough time for them to write the answers in the participant book.

3. Or, take some time at the beginning of the class session for group members to work individually. Have them read the Dimension One questions and the Scripture references and then write their answers to the questions in the spaces provided in the participant book. Discuss together any questions or answers in Dimension One that do not seem clear. This approach may take longer than the others, but it provides a good change of pace from time to time.

You do not have to organize your class sessions the same way every week. Ask the class members what they prefer. Experiment! You may find ways to study the Dimension One material other than the ones listed above.

The second part of each lesson in this leader guide corresponds to the second part of the participant book lessons. The Dimension Two section of the participant book provides background information to help the participants understand the Scripture. Become familiar with the information in the participant book.

Dimension Two of this leader guide contains additional information on the passage. The leader guide goes into more depth with some parts of the passage than the participant book does. You will want to share this information with the group in whatever way seems appropriate. For example, if someone raises a question about a particular verse, share any additional background information from the leader guide.

You might raise a simple question such as, What words or phrases gave you trouble in understanding the passage? or, Having grasped the content of the passage, what questions remain in your mind? Encourage the group members to share confusing points, troublesome words or phrases, or lingering questions. Write these problems on a posterboard or markerboard. This list of concerns will form the outline for the second portion of the session.

These concerns may also stimulate some research on the part of the group members. If your study group is large enough, divide the class into three groups. Then divide the passage for the following week into three parts. Assign a portion of the passage to each group. Using Bible commentaries and Bible dictionaries, direct each group to discover as much as it can about this portion of the passage before the class meets again. Each group will then report its findings during the class session.

The third part of each lesson in this leader guide relates to Dimension Three in the participant book. This section helps class members discover how to apply the Scripture to their own lives. Here you will find one or more interpretations of the passage—whether traditional, historical, or contemporary. Use these interpretations when appropriate to illumine the passage for the group members.

Dimension Three in the participant book points out some of the issues in the passage that are relevant to our lives. For each of these issues, the participant book raises questions to help the participants assess the meaning of the Scripture for their lives. The information in Dimension Three of the leader guide is designed to help you lead the class in discussing these issues. Usually, you will find a more in-depth discussion of portions of the Scripture.

The discussion in the leader guide will give you a better perspective on the Scripture and its interpretation before you begin to assess its meaning for today. You will probably want to share this Dimension Three information with the class to open the discussion. For each life situation, the leader guide contains suggestions on facilitating the class discussion. You, as the leader, are responsible for group discussions of Dimension Three issues.

Assembling Your Materials

You will need at least three items to prepare for and conduct each class session:

- A leader guide

- A participant book

- A Bible—you may use any translation or several; the answers in this leader guide are taken from the New International Version.

One advantage of the Genesis to Revelation Series is that the study is self-contained. That is, all you need to lead this Bible study is provided for you in the participant books and leader guides. Occasionally, or perhaps on a regular basis, you might want to consult other sources for additional information.

HOW TO LEAD A DISCUSSION

The Teacher as Discussion Leader

As the leader of this series or a part of this series, one of your main responsibilities during each class period will be to lead the class discussion. Some leaders are apprehensive about leading a discussion. In many ways, it is easier to lecture to the class. But remember that the class members will surely benefit more from the class sessions when they actively participate in a discussion of the material.

Leading a discussion is a skill that any teacher can master with practice. And keep in mind—especially if your class is not used to discussion—that the members of your group will also be learning through practice. The following are some pointers on how to lead interesting and thought-provoking discussions in the study group.

Preparing for a Discussion—Where Do I Start?

1. Focus on the subject that will be discussed and on the goal you want to achieve through that discussion.

2. Prepare by collecting information and data that you will need; jot down these ideas, facts, and questions so that you will have them when you need them.

3. Begin organizing your ideas; stop often to review your work. Keep in mind the climate within the group—attitudes, feelings, eagerness to participate and learn.

4. Consider possible alternative group procedures. Be prepared for the unexpected.

5. Having reached your goal, think through several ways to bring the discussion to a close.

As the leader, do not feel that your responsibility is to give a full account or report of the assigned material. This practice promotes dependency. Instead, through stimulating questions and discussion, the participants will read the material—not because you tell them to but because they want to read and prepare.

How Do I Establish a Climate for Learning?

The leader's readiness and preparation quickly establish a climate in which the group can proceed and its members learn and grow. The anxiety and fear of an unprepared leader are contagious but so are the positive vibrations coming from a leader who is prepared to move into a learning enterprise.

An attitude of shared ownership is also basic. Group members need to perceive themselves as part of the learning experience. Persons establish ownership by working on goals, sharing concerns, and accepting major responsibility for learning.

Here are several ways the leader can foster a positive climate for learning and growth.

1. Readiness. A leader who is always fully prepared can promote, in turn, the group's readiness to learn.

2. Exploration. When the leader encourages group members to freely explore new ideas, persons will know they are in a group whose primary function is learning.

3. Exposure. A leader who is open, honest, and willing to reveal himself or herself to the group will encourage participants to discuss their feelings and opinions.

4. Confidentiality. A leader can create a climate for learning when he or she respects the confidentiality of group members and encourages the group members to respect one another's confidentiality.

5. Acceptance. When a leader shows a high degree of acceptance, participants can likewise accept one another honestly.

How Can I Deal With Conflict?

What if conflict or strong disagreement arises in your group? What do you do? Think about the effective and ineffective ways you have dealt with conflict in the past.

Group conflict may come from one of several sources. One common source of conflict involves personality clashes. Any group is almost certain to contain at least two persons whose personalities clash. If you break your class into smaller groups for discussion, be sure these persons are in separate groups.

Another common source of group conflict is subject matter. The Bible can be a very controversial subject. Remember the difference between discussion or disagreement and conflict. As a leader you will have to decide when to encourage discussion and when to discourage conflict that is destructive to the group process.

Group conflict may also come from a general atmosphere conducive to expression of ideas and opinions. Try to discourage persons in the group from being judgmental toward others and their ideas. Keep reminding the class that each person is entitled to his or her own opinions and that no one opinion is more valid than another.

How Much Should I Contribute to the Discussion?

Many leaders are unsure about how much they should contribute to the class discussions. Below are several pitfalls to avoid.

1. The leader should remain neutral on a question until the group has had adequate time to discuss it. At the proper time in the discussion the leader can offer his or her opinion. The leader can direct the questions to the group at large, rechanneling those questions that come to him or her.

    At times when the members need to grapple with a question or issue, the most untimely response a leader can make is answering the question. Do not fall into the trap of doing the group members' work for them. Let them struggle with the question.

    However, if the leader has asked the group members to reveal thoughts and feelings, then group members have the right to expect the same of the leader. A leader has no right to ask others to reveal something he or she is unwilling to reveal. A leader can reveal thoughts and feelings, but at the appropriate time.

    The refusal to respond immediately to a question often takes self-discipline. The leader has spent time thinking, reading, and preparing. Thus the leader usually does have a point of view, and waiting for others to respond calls for restraint.

2. Another pitfall is the leader's making a speech or extended comments in expressing an opinion or summarizing what has been said. For example, in an attempt to persuade others, a leader may speak, repeat, or strongly emphasize what someone says concerning a question.

3. Finally, the pitfall of believing the leader must know "the answers" to the questions is always apparent. The leader need not know all the answers. Many questions that should be raised are ultimate and unanswerable; other questions are open-ended; and still others have several answers.

GENESIS TO REVELATION SERIES
MINOR PROPHETS
Leader Guide

Table of Contents

About the Writer

Dr. Gene M. Tucker, the writer of these lessons on the Minor Prophets, served as Professor of Old Testament Studies at Candler School of Theology, Emory University in Atlanta, Georgia. He wrote many books and articles in the field of biblical studies.

Hear the word of the Lord, you Israelites, / because the Lord has a charge to bring / against you who live in the land. (4:1)

HOSEA'S FAMILY AND GOD'S WORD

Hosea 1–6

DIMENSION ONE: WHAT DOES THE BIBLE SAY?

Answer these questions by reading Hosea 1

1. What is the Lord's first command to Hosea? (1:2)

    The Lord first commands Hosea to take an adulterous wife and then to have children of unfaithfulness with her.

2. Who is Hosea's wife? (1:3)

    Gomer is Hosea's wife.

3. What does the Lord tell Hosea to name his first son, and why? (1:4)

    Hosea must name his first son Jezreel, because God will punish the house of Jehu for the massacre at Jezreel.

4. What is the name of the prophet's daughter, and why? (1:6)

    Hosea must call his daughter Lo-Ruhamah ("not loved" or "not pitied"). This name signifies that God will no longer have pity on or show love to the house of Israel.

5. What does God tell Hosea to name his third child, and why? (1:9)

God declares that Hosea must name his third child Lo-Ammi ("not my people"). This name signifies that the people of Israel are not God's people, and the Lord is not their God.

6. What will the people of Israel be called? (1:10)

The people of Israel will be called "children of the living God."

Answer these questions by reading Hosea 2

7. What is Hosea to ask Gomer to do? (2:2)

Hosea is to ask Gomer to put away her adultery and unfaithfulness.

8. What did the wife (Israel) not acknowledge? (2:8)

The wife did not acknowledge who gave her the grain, the wine, the oil, the silver, and the gold that was used to worship Baal.

9. Who is speaking in Hosea 2:9-13? (2:13)

God is speaking.

10. In the future, what will Israel (the wife) say to the Lord? (2:16)

In the future, Israel will address the Lord as "my husband."

11. How will the Lord betroth Israel in the future? (2:19-20)

In the future, the Lord will betroth Israel in righteousness, justice, love, compassion, and faithfulness.

Answer these questions by reading Hosea 3

12. Why does the Lord command Hosea to love a woman, even though she is an adulteress? (3:1)

The prophet's love for Gomer parallels God's love for Israel.

13. Is the adulterous woman named in chapter 3? (3:1-5)

    The name of the woman is not given; it may be Gomer.

14. What will the Israelites do after God takes them back? (3:5)

    The Israelites will return and seek their God, their king, and come trembling to the Lord.

Answer these questions by reading Hosea 4

15. Why does the Lord have a charge to bring against the inhabitants of the land? (4:1-2)

    The inhabitants are not faithful or kind. They do not know God. They curse, lie, murder, steal, commit adultery, and bloodshed follows bloodshed.

16. Who is addressed in Hosea 4:4-10? (4:4)

    The priests are addressed in Hosea 4:4-10.

17. What do the people "consult," and what has led them astray? (4:12)

    The people consult a wooden idol; a spirit of prostitution has led them astray.

18. Who will be punished when the daughters turn to prostitution and the daughters-in-law commit adultery, and why? (4:14)

    God will punish the fathers and the husbands, because they consort with harlots and sacrifice with shrine prostitutes.

Answer these questions by reading Hosea 5

19. What does not permit the people of Ephraim to return to their God, and why? (5:4)

    Their deeds do not permit the people of Ephraim to return to their God. A spirit of prostitution is within them, and they do not acknowledge the Lord.

20. What is the Lord like to Ephraim and Judah? (5:12)

    The Lord is like a moth to Ephraim and like rot to Judah.

21. What did Ephraim do when he saw his sickness? (5:13)

    He turned to Assyria and sent to the great king for help.

22. What does the Lord expect the people to do? (5:15)

    They should acknowledge guilt and seek God.

Answer these questions by reading Hosea 6

23. What does the Lord desire? (6:6)

    The Lord desires mercy, not sacrifice, and acknowledgment of God rather than burnt offerings.

24. What is the "horrible thing," in the house of Israel? (6:10)

    The horrible thing in the house of Israel is Ephraim's prostitution and defilement.

DIMENSION TWO:
WHAT DOES THE BIBLE MEAN?

Introduction to Hosea. The Book of Hosea has two distinct parts. One part consists of accounts and speeches concerning the family life of the prophet (chs. 1–3). The other part is a series of prophetic speeches (chs. 4–14). This lesson includes all of the first part and the beginning of the second. The chapters about the prophet's family, though related to one another, are quite distinct. Chapter 1 is a third-person report about God's command to Hosea. Hosea is to take "an adulterous wife" and have "children of unfaithfulness." The prophet fulfills that command. Chapter 2 is a lawsuit against an unfaithful wife. The account is in a poetic form. Chapter 3 is a first-person account by the prophet of God's command to love a woman who is an adulteress. The speeches in chapters 4–6 are mainly indictments or prophecies of punishment against the people of Israel. Some are addressed to specific groups of the people, such as the priests.

Hosea's Time and Circumstances. Immediately after stressing that the prophet's words come from God, the first verse of the book gives Hosea's dates and the name of his father. This information does not simply satisfy historical curiosity. It expresses a conviction that is basic to the Old Testament: the word of God comes through real human beings in history. While that word will continue to have significance for later generations, it was spoken first for the prophet's own time.

When was Hosea active? Hosea 1:1 gives an answer, but it is partial and not without problems. For example, only one northern king, Jeroboam, is listed. Jeroboam's reign corresponds only to that of the first Judean king listed, Uzziah. But on the basis of other information in the book, the approximate dates of Hosea can be established. He prophesied from 750 BC (the last years of Jeroboam's reign) to just before the fall of Samaria. Samaria, the capital of Israel, fell to the Assyrians in 722–721 BC. Hosea was a contemporary of Isaiah and Micah, and a younger contemporary of Amos. He was active for thirty years. Unfortunately, we have no information about the end of his life or prophetic work.

Most of Hosea's prophetic activity was carried out during a time of political chaos. Assyria was an ever-increasing threat. Israel was in conflict with even Judah. In the last few years before the fall, Israel had one revolt after another. Often the prophet was called to speak directly to political issues, including criticism of the king.

Hosea is the only prophet of the Northern Kingdom whose words have come to us in a book. Amos preached in the North, but he was from the South. You may want to use a map to show the geographical features of Israel in relation to Judah during this period.

The geographical features of the North created some special religious problems. Judah's terrain was made of rough hills and semi-desert, suitable mainly for grazing herds and vineyards. While the South (Judah) was more isolated, the North (Israel) was more open to outside contacts and influence. Israel's farmland was richer, and the people were more oriented to agriculture. They were more urban and more cosmopolitan than Judah. Consequently, it is not surprising that the Canaanite fertility cult seemed to thrive in Israel.

According to the prophets of Israel, the people kept asking themselves, "Who makes our land fertile, Baal or the Lord?" Elijah and Elisha had faced that question a century earlier. But it persisted, and became the main focus of Hosea's message.

Unfortunately, we have few details concerning Canaanite religion in the time of Hosea. From evidence within the Old Testament, and from other ancient texts, it appears that the religion of the non-Israelite people focused on fertility. The myths of Baal and other deities, such as Asherah and El, told how their activities assured the fertility of the earth and all living things on it. Baal himself was a storm god. He was often pictured with a spear that represents lightning.

The Marriage of Hosea. The first three chapters of Hosea present serious problems for interpreters. Many readers have found it troubling that God should command a prophet to marry a prostitute, an immoral act in ancient Israel. Do these three chapters mean to report actual events in the life of the prophet or not?

Some early Christian and Jewish interpreters regarded the references to the prophet's marriage and family as allegorical. These interpreters thought they were not actual events but stories told to represent deeper realities. Others argued that Hosea simply reports a dream or a vision. Neither of these explanations is likely. The Old Testament accounts unfold as the direct reports of events. When the prophets report visions or allegories, they always share them as such.

Most modern interpreters see all three chapters as biographical or autobiographical. These chapters tell how the prophet learned the love of God through his own painful marriage. "An adulterous wife" is taken to mean that Gomer was not an actual prostitute when Hosea married her, but that she had such tendencies. Later on she went astray, and the prophet found her and brought her back. One problem with this view is that it assumes the woman in chapter 3 is the Gomer of chapter 1. That may be the case, but the Bible itself does not say so.

These chapters are reports of symbolic actions by the prophet, actual events performed to bring God's word to life. According to Hosea 1:2, the prophet knew the word of God before his marriage and before he gave his children their symbolic names. Similar reports of symbolic actions are found in 2 Kings 13:14-19; Isaiah 7:14; 8:1-4; Jeremiah 19:12. Suggest that different members of the group read these other passages and compare them with Hosea 1–3.

The prophet saw his marriage and family life as the result of his understanding of God's word, not as the cause of his message. Gomer, as a wife of harlotry, represented unfaithful Israel. She probably participated in the Canaanite fertility cult, just as most other Israelites did. Hosea's message is not that his wife and family are so unusual, but the reverse; all Israelites have sold themselves to the worship of false gods.

Hosea 1:2-9. These verses include a command to the prophet and the report of how the command was fulfilled. The general command (v. 2) also gives the reasons for the actions. The people have forsaken God. The report of Hosea's obedience has three parts, corresponding to the birth of the three children. The account moves from accusation and threat of punishment (vv. 4-5), to God's withdrawal of forgiveness (v. 6), to the announcement that the covenant between Israel and God has ended (v. 9).

With the exception of verse 7, these verses announce judgment upon Israel. Moreover, the prophet and his family are by no means exempted from that judgment. They are identified with the sinful and condemned people.

Hosea 1:10-11. This paragraph comments on the future. Because its style and form are unusual, it may not come from Hosea himself. However, the comment in no way contradicts the harsh message of the children's names. It sees past the judgment day to a time of salvation when the covenant will be renewed.

Hosea 2:1-13. The prophet, speaking on behalf of God, accuses his wife (who represents Israel) of unfaithfulness. The section follows the pattern of a trial. The children are called as witnesses. It moves from indictment to evidence to announcement of the punishment (vv. 9-13). The punishment includes public ridicule, the end of all religious practices and celebrations, and the destruction of vineyards and orchards.

Hosea 2:14-15. The prophet recalls the time of the wilderness wandering as a period when Israel was young and faithful. The Lord will take Israel back into the desert so that the people can learn that God is the source of all they have.

Hosea 2:16-23. These verses combine the traditional language of the covenant with the vocabulary of love. The words describe the relationship between God and Israel. That the prophet refers to God as the husband of Israel is quite remarkable. He resorts to all possible human analogies to point to the depth and intimacy of the love between God and people. The new covenant will be broad enough to include all living things. It will be deep enough to establish righteousness and justice. The Lord will take the initiative, thus enabling the people to know God.

Hosea 3:1-5. This chapter is a first-person account (ch. 1 is in the third person). This chapter tells of a symbolic action in two parts. It gives the account of the command (v. 1) and its fulfillment. We see from the command that the purchase of the woman is to show that God continues to love Israel in spite of the people's unfaithfulness. God will deprive the people of leaders and religious practices so that that they will eventually return to their God.

Hosea 4:1-3. Like the lawsuit against the unfaithful wife in Hosea 2, this section follows the pattern of a trial. The word translated *charge* is a term for a lawsuit. After issuing a summons to the people, the prophet presents a general, and then a specific, indictment. The general indictment states their failures. The people show no faithfulness, kindness or knowledge of God. The specific indictment lists five particular crimes that correspond to half of the Ten Commandments (Exodus 20:2-17; Deuteronomy 5:6-21). Behind this list stands a tradition of the law in relation to the covenant. The people know what they are expected to do.

Hosea 4:4-10. This speech, like the one that precedes it, begins as a lawsuit. The accusation and announcement of punishment are addressed to the priests of Israel. They have failed in one of their central responsibilities, teaching the law to the laity. The word *knowledge* means teaching and learning the content of the law. The prophet also accuses the priests of greed and of participating in the sin of all the people: prostitution.

Hosea 4:11-14. Israel's harlotry is not simply a matter of belief, feeling, or apathy toward God. It entails certain specific actions. As used here, the word *consult* is a technical term for acts of divination. The people consult idols or other pagan cult objects to determine the future. They sacrifice at places usually identified with Canaanite gods such as Baal.

The terms *prostitution* and *adultery* occur several times in this section. The terms do not refer to ordinary prostitution. In verse 12, the image represents Israel's apostasy. The allusions in verse 14 refer quite specifically to cultic prostitution. Cultic prostitution included sexual acts performed as a part of the fertility cult. The problem must have been an acute one in ancient Israel. Deuteronomy 23:17-18 prohibits cultic prostitution and makes it illegal to bring money earned by prostitutes into the house of the Lord.

Hosea 4:15-19. The indictment of Israel continues. The prophet tells the people to avoid Gilgal and Beth Aven. These are two of the best-known sanctuaries of the Northern Kingdom. Gilgal is mentioned in Joshua 4:19. Beth Aven (literally, "house of evil") is an insulting name for Bethel. The apostasy of the people apparently was not limited to their worship at pagan sanctuaries. It included false worship at centers dedicated to God. The prophet says that their worship is idolatrous.

Hosea 5:1-7. In verses 2 and 3, the "I" seems to be the Lord. But elsewhere (vv. 4-7) the prophet speaks about "the LORD." The first two verses call the priests, the house of Israel, and the house of the king to hear. They give reasons for punishment, and announce that punishment will come. Verses 3-5 give the familiar indictment that Israel is guilty of harlotry. Verses 6-7 announce that God will withdraw from them, and they will suffer.

Hosea 5:8-14. The historical background of this passage probably is the Syro-Ephraimitic war (734 BC). This war is mentioned also in Isaiah 7 and 2 Kings 15:27-30. Israel and other states in the region formed an alliance against the Assyrian Empire, but Judah refused to join. Israel then mounted a campaign to the south to force Judah to join the revolt. Judah countered by establishing a treaty with the Assyrians. Hosea says that foreign alliances will not save the people.

Hosea 5:15–6:6. This section begins with a speech of the Lord (5:15). A penitential song of the people follows. In Hosea 6:4-6, God speaks again, in response to the song. If 6:4-6 interprets the song of the people, their repentance does not seem sincere. Their repentance is "like the early dew that disappears." Can you tell from reading these verses whether the penitential song is sincere or shallow? You may wish to discuss with the group some of the marks of true confession and repentance according to the prophets. The key to the passage, and to the question of true repentance, seems to be Hosea 6:6. True faith is not revealed by acts of worship (sacrifice and burnt offerings). Steadfast love and the knowledge of God are marks of true faith.

Hosea 6:7-11. The meaning of the phrase *at Adam* is uncertain. It probably does not refer to Adam and the garden of Eden. The phrase could mean "like men," that is every one of them. However, since it is in a context that refers to places, it probably refers to a town. Gilead is on the eastern side of the Jordan.

DIMENSION THREE: WHAT DOES THE BIBLE MEAN TO ME?

The Relationship Between God and People

The heart of Hosea's message concerns the deep and intimate relationship between God and Israel. Focus on this theme and its relationship to our lives of faith by asking the group to list the images for that divine-human relationship that appear in the first six chapters.

Some of these images were traditional in the time of Hosea. Most speak in terms of the covenant, the laws given with the covenant, and the history of God's acts of salvation toward Israel. Hosea does not introduce any new laws. He assumes that the people already know what response was expected of them as a covenant people. We saw in Dimension Two how Hosea refers to the Ten Commandments in 4:2. While the prophet does not state it explicitly, when he accuses the people of being unfaithful to God, he assumes another commandment, the first one: "You shall have no other gods before me" (Exodus 20:3). How important are laws, rules, and regulations in relationships, and especially the relationship between God and people?

Probably more difficult to understand and appreciate than the traditional ways of characterizing the relationship between God and people are the new and distinctive images in Hosea. Most of these use the intimate vocabulary of family life. Especially in the first three chapters, the prophet describes the relationship, at both its best and its worst, as like that of a husband and a wife.

Give the group members an opportunity to react to this way of speaking of God. The problem behind this language is the difficulty of finding words to speak of God. The prophets, and all biblical writers, were limited in the same way that we are. They had to seek human words and images to point to their understanding of what is beyond human words and images. Hosea had experienced God as passionately concerned with Israel. He saw God as angry and frustrated, like a husband with a faithless wife. He saw God as seeking ways to restore the relationship of love. Thus he used the language of marriage, divorce, and even courtship as analogies for the way of

God with Israel. And he used prostitution (or harlotry or whoredom) and adultery as analogies for Israel's way with God.

Discuss with the group the questions posed in the participant book concerning the good news of the Book of Hosea, that one day God will restore the relationship with the people.

Faithfulness and Morality

Hosea speaks constantly of Israel's sins and crimes. He names specific violations of laws, and almost cites chapter and verse. But he knows the difference between corporate sin and individual sins. For Hosea, one problem leads to all the others, Israel's unfaithfulness to God. Because they are not faithful to their God, the people commit one crime after another.

The most frequent word for Israel's unfaithfulness is *prostitution*. At the heart of this expression is the prophet's accusation that the people have failed to give total allegiance to God, and instead have worshiped Baal. Because of this prostitution, there has been actual prostitution, both sacred and secular, and even violent crimes including murder.

Discuss with the group the difference between *sin* and individual *sins*, and the issue of the relationship between faithfulness and morality. Do a person's deepest commitments, whether to God or to various false gods, determine his or her behavior?

Along with the strong language for Israel's unfaithfulness, there is also the rich vocabulary for faithfulness. Human faithfulness is possible for the Old Testament writers, because God is trustworthy and faithful. Thus God expects Israel to know that God shows steadfast love. God acts with justice, righteousness, and mercy.

Close today's session by asking group members to reflect upon the insights they have gained from their study of Hosea 1–6. Ask them to pose questions about the message of the prophet that they would like to consider as they study Hosea 7–14. If time allows, list the insights and questions on markerboard or a large sheet of paper.

How can I give you up, Ephraim? / How can I hand you over, Israel? . . . / all my compassion is aroused. (11:8)

GOD'S WRATH AND COMPASSION

Hosea 7–14

DIMENSION ONE: WHAT DOES THE BIBLE SAY?

Answer these questions by reading Hosea 7

1. When the Lord would heal Israel, what is exposed? (7:1)

   The sins of Ephraim and the crimes of Samaria are revealed.

2. How do the people delight the king and princes? (7:3)

   They delight the king and princes with their wickedness and their lies.

3. Who calls upon the Lord? (7:7)

   No one calls upon the Lord.

4. What testifies against Ephraim? (7:10)

   The arrogance of Israel testifies against Ephraim.

5. What do the people do instead of crying out to the Lord from the heart? (7:14-16)

   The people wail upon their beds, gather together (or slash themselves) for grain and new wine, and turn away from the Lord.

Answer these questions by reading Hosea 8

6. Why is an eagle ("vulture" in the NRSV) over the house of Israel? (8:1)

Israel has broken God's covenant and rebelled against the divine law.

7. What will happen to the calf of Samaria? (8:6)

The calf of Samaria will be broken in pieces.

8. Why is Israel swallowed up and like a worthless thing? (8:8-9)

Israel is swallowed up and like a worthless thing, because the people of Israel have gone up to Assyria and sold themselves to lovers.

9. What is God about to do, and why? (8:13-14)

God will remember their wickedness, punish their sins, and return them to Egypt, because Israel has forgotten God and built palaces. Because Judah has fortified many cities, God will send fire upon them.

Answer these questions by reading Hosea 9

10. Where is Israel to go? (9:3)

Israel will not remain in the land of the Lord, but will return to Egypt and eat unclean food in Assyria.

11. How is the prophet characterized? (9:7-8)

The prophet is considered a fool and a maniac, but the prophet is watchman for God's people.

12. Where did Israel become vile, and how? (9:10)

Israel became vile at Baal Peor, because the people consecrated themselves to Baal.

13. What will God do to the people of Israel, and why? (9:17)

God will reject the people of Israel, and they shall become wanderers, because they have not obeyed God.

Answer these questions by reading Hosea 10

14. How does Israel make promises and agreements? (10:4)

    Israel makes promises with false oaths.

15. What will happen to the king in Samaria and to the high places of wickedness? (10:7-8)

    The king will perish, and the high places of wickedness will be destroyed.

16. What should Israel do, and why? (10:12)

    God calls for Israel to sow righteousness, reap the fruit of unfailing love, break up the unplowed ground, and seek the Lord.

Answer these questions by reading Hosea 11

17. Who is speaking the words recorded in Hosea 11:1-9?

    God is speaking these words.

18. How does God describe Israel, and what does that suggest about the nature of God? (11:1)

    God describes Israel as a son, suggesting that the Lord is a loving parent.

19. What did the Lord do for Ephraim? (11:3-4)

    The Lord taught Ephraim to walk, took them by the arms, led them with cords of human kindness and ties of love, lifted the yoke from their necks, and bent down to feed them.

20. How are God's words in verses 8-9 different from those in verses 5-7? (11:5-9)

    In contrast with God's harsh, angry, and threatening words in verses 5-7, the words in verses 8-9 are warm, loving, and forgiving.

21. Why will God not devastate Ephraim? (11:9)

    God will not carry out fierce anger or again devastate Ephraim, because God is the Holy One, not human.

Answer these questions by reading Hosea 12

22. What does it mean that Ephraim "feeds on the wind" and "pursues the east wind"? (12:1)

It means that Ephraim multiplies lies and violence, and makes a treaty with Assyria and with Egypt.

23. How does the Lord speak to and through the prophets? (12:10)

The Lord speaks to and through the prophets in visions and parables.

24. How did God bring Israel from Egypt? (12:13)

God brought Israel up from Egypt and cared for the people through a prophet.

Answer these questions by reading Hosea 13

25. How does Ephraim sin more and more? (13:2)

Ephraim sins more and more by making silver images and idols and calling for people to sacrifice to them. They kiss the calf-idols.

26. What relationship does God have with Israel? (13:4-5)

God is Israel's God, the only God they are to know, beside whom there is no Savior. God cared for them in the desert, after they escaped Egypt.

27. What will happen to Samaria, and why? (13:16)

Because Samaria has rebelled against God, Samaria shall bear its guilt. The people shall fall by the sword, their little ones will be dashed to the ground, and pregnant women ripped open.

Answer these questions by reading Hosea 14

28. What does the prophet instruct the people to do? (14:1)

The prophet calls upon the people to return to the Lord.

29. What is the wise and discerning person to do? (14:9)

This person will understand and realize ""these things" (apparently referring to the Book of Hosea) because God's ways are right. The righteous walk in God's ways, but the rebellious stumble in them.

DIMENSION TWO:
WHAT DOES THE BIBLE MEAN?

Background. As we noted in lesson 1, the Book of Hosea consists of two distinct sections. Chapters 1–3 contain reports and speeches concerning the prophet's family. Chapters 4–14 are a collection of prophetic speeches. This lesson takes up the last part of the collection of speeches. In terms of form, most of them are presented as direct quotations of the Lord. In some of them, though, the prophet presents himself as the speaker. In terms of content, most are accusations against the people or prophecies of punishment, though some are announcements of salvation.

Finding the Units. As the participant book notes, Hosea 7:1-2 continues a speech that began either in 6:11b or 6:7. What seems to be a small matter raises a question of great importance for understanding the Old Testament prophetic books. How do we know when a speech or narrative begins or ends? The chapter and verse numbers do not necessarily indicate the original units. They were added long after the books were written.

Presumably, most of the present prophetic books record the original oral speeches of the prophets. Finding the units is one way of recovering the form of the original speeches. But this process also helps to make sense of the text. Where does a message, or a part of a message, begin and end? One way of recognizing the units is the appearance of introductory or concluding formulas, such as "Hear the word of the LORD" (4:1). But the Book of Hosea, unlike most other early prophetic books, has very few such formulas. Another way is to notice the change of speaker (prophet or the Lord) or addressee (the people or a special group), or changes in mood, tone, or content (from bad news to good).

Hosea 7:1-2. In Hosea, *Israel* refers to the Northern Kingdom and not to the nation as a whole, as it sometimes does elsewhere in the Old Testament. *Ephraim*, originally the name of one of the northern tribes, is used as a synonym for Israel. *Samaria* was the capital city of the Northern Kingdom, and often stands for the nation as well.

Hosea 7:3-7. This passage addresses some of the problems of Israel's political life. It speaks of the sins of the monarchy and the political intrigues of persons in high places. The "day of the festival of our king" (v. 5) must refer to a special celebration, possibly a coronation day or its anniversary. During the celebration, conspirators overthrow the king. Because of such activities, the monarchy is doomed. The realistic background of this prophetic speech is the series of palace revolts in the last decades of Israel's existence before the final capture of Samaria by the Assyrians in 722/21 BC.

Hosea 7:10. See also 7:11, 14. The expressions *return*, *search*, *call*, and *cry* refer not only to a change of heart or feeling toward God. They also describe specific actions, including public worship, prayer, and formal inquiry concerning the will of God.

Hosea 7:13-16. The precise meaning of the Hebrew word translated *woe* (v. 13) is uncertain. But its force in prophetic speeches is all too clear. The cry is usually followed by a description of the sins of a group of people and sometimes, as here, by an announcement of judgment against them. The word may have been taken over by the prophets from the mourning cry at Israelite funerals. The words *rebel* or *turn away* (vv. 13, 14) are translated from one of the Hebrew words for sin. One of the sins is that people "slash themselves" for grain and wine (v. 14, but see footnote). This alludes to a fertility ritual in the worship of Baal, who was thought to provide grain and wine. The account of the contest between Elijah and the prophets of Baal on Mount Carmel (1 Kings 18) describes the practice. This practice is prohibited in Deuteronomy 14:1 and Leviticus 19:28.

Hosea 8:1-3. Though *covenant* is one of the central ideas of the Old Testament, the prophets seldom use the term as such. At this point, Hosea uses *law* as a synonym for *covenant.* Another aspect of the concept is made clear in Hosea 10:4. Here the people are accused of making covenants with "false oaths." In the Old Testament, a covenant was a solemn, sworn agreement, a promise established by an oath. Such agreements were made between individuals or as treaties between nations. The covenant of Sinai was the foundational agreement between the Lord and the people. The Lord promised to be their God, and they promised to be the people of God. The "law" was the content of the sworn agreement of the people, what they promised to do as their part of the covenant. Thus the laws in Exodus 20–23 are called the "Book of the Covenant" (Exodus 24:7). Hosea must have been very familiar with the traditions concerning the covenant at Sinai and the laws associated with it. In 13:4, he cites the beginning of the Ten Commandments (Exodus 20:1-17), and in 4:2 he refers to some of the laws.

Hosea 8:4-14. In this section, God speaks. God links the corruption of the monarchy with idolatry. The institution of kingship is beset with problems, because the people "set up kings without my consent" (v. 4). Hosea often criticizes kings and the kingship (see 7:3, 7; 8:10; 9:15; 10:3, 7, 15; 13:10).

Hosea's attitude toward the monarchy brings out an important difference between attitudes toward the institution in Israel and Judah. In contrast to the northern prophet Hosea, the Judean prophets Isaiah and Micah hold more positive views of the monarchy. In the South, there was a strong belief that God had promised to David that one of his sons would always sit on the throne in Jerusalem (2 Samuel 7). Consequently, from the time of David to the Babylonian Exile, there was stability in Judah, and few serious challenges to the dynasty of David. In the Northern Kingdom, however, there was no such belief. No dynasty was secure. The series of palace revolutions in Israel during the time of Hosea were part of a long tradition.

According to this passage, the domestic or internal corruption of Israel and its leaders is idolatry (vv. 4, 5, 11). The international or external political evil is the establishment of treaties with foreign powers (vv. 8-10). God promises to punish these sins. God will destroy the idols (vv. 4- 5). Israel will be punished by military defeat (vv. 8, 14) and exile to Egypt (v. 13).

Hosea 9:1-6. The form of these verses is direct address. The form and the references to specific rituals suggest that the prophet delivered this speech to a group. They were probably assembled for a religious festival. The purpose of the festival would have been thanksgiving and renewal of life. The songs, prayers, and sacrifices were probably directed to God. But Hosea accuses the people of harlotry and forsaking God (v. 1). He announces punishment as the end of such celebrations as well as exile.

Hosea 9:7-9. Hosea encountered great hatred (v. 7) from the people and from official religious leaders (v. 8). But like other prophets, he was able to endure such animosity because he saw himself as a watchman (see also Jeremiah 6:17; Ezekiel 3:16-21; 33:7-9). Does Hosea understand himself as a watchman on behalf of Israel, guarding them from harm, or on behalf of God, watching for unfaithfulness?

Hosea 9:10-17. God, through the prophet, takes up again the theme of the sojourn in the desert in the time of Moses. This passage reflects the dual themes of the account of the wilderness wandering: God's care for Israel and the people's rebellion. "Baal Peor" is a reference to the tradition preserved in Numbers 25:1-18, which reports how the people gave themselves to Baal of Peor. The curse that there will be "no birth, no pregnancy, no conception" is a reversal of the expected benefits of worshiping a fertility god. Gilgal (v. 15) was an important place during the period of the conquest (Joshua 5:9-10). Saul's kingship also began there (1 Samuel 11:14-15). The passage may simply refer to the contemporary worship at its sanctuary, however.

Hosea 10:1-8. As in Hosea 8:4-14, the prophet connects the sin of dependence on a human king with the sin of idolatry. Both kings and idols will be destroyed. God will break down the altars and pillars, remove the calf of Beth Aven, and destroy the high places of Aven. The people will be forced to live without a king, for "Samaria's king will be swept away" (v. 7).

Hosea 10:9-10. These verses are in the typical form of a prophecy of punishment. God is the speaker. The speech begins with a general and broad indictment directed against Israel (v. 9) and their history of sin. Following is the announcement of punishment, God's own promise to act against the wayward people. As a result, "nations will be gathered against them" (v. 10).

Hosea 10:11-12. Hosea, like most other Old Testament prophets, frequently uses the terms *righteousness* and *unfailing love* to characterize what God expects of Israel. Righteousness frequently parallels justice. Unfailing love describes the relationship expected in the covenant. This love is enduring devotion to God.

Hosea 10:13-15. In order to communicate the severity of the military defeat God plans for Israel, the prophet alludes to the destruction of the city of Beth Arbel by Shalman (v. 14). The city, the conqueror, and the event would have been well known to Hosea's audience, but none of them has been identified with certainty.

Hosea 11:1-11. This section is one of the most important and compelling passages in the entire Old Testament. Ask the members of the group to identify the speaker and the addressee. The Lord is the speaker, except in verse 10, but who is addressed? Direct address appears only in verse 8. Then ask the group to consider whether these verses comprise a single unit, only part of a larger section, or several originally separate speeches. What, for example, is the relationship of the announcements of salvation in verses 8-9 and 10-11 to the announcement of judgment in verses 5-7? What is the relationship of the review of past relationships in verses 1-4 to the remainder? Does a speech end with verse 11 or with verse 12? Then ask the group to define the message of the unit. Is the news for Israel good or bad?

Most modern commentators take 11:1-11 to be a single speech. These verses are a divine soliloquy on God's relationship to Israel and its future. God is pictured as ambivalent, undecided about what to do. The people have been unfaithful and deserve judgment. But the metaphors at the beginning have already established the basis for a different outcome. God's care for Israel has always been like that of a parent for a child. God's compassion is beyond even that: "I will not carry out my fierce anger . . . I for I am God, and not a man" (v. 9).

Israel is described as God's "son" (see also 13:13). We should not rush to the conclusion that God is viewed here strictly as a male father figure; mothers have sons, too. We can communicate an understanding of One who is more than human only through the use of human language. Hosea uses a great many highly personal images to point toward the nature of God. God is like a husband, or even a lover, to Israel; or one who treats Israel like a father treats a son. Moreover, the images in this passage are as maternal as they are paternal. *Compassion* (see v. 8) in the Old Testament suggests female rather than masculine imagery. God's compassion for Israel is like that of a mother for her child and even beyond it.

Hosea 12:2-6. That they had the Book of Genesis in its present form is unlikely, but both Hosea and his audience knew much about the patriarchs. Here, Hosea alludes to the story of Jacob's birth (Genesis 25:21-26), to his brother Esau, to the tradition of his struggle with God, and the change of his name to Israel (Genesis 32:22-32), and to the account of his dream at Bethel (Genesis 28:11-17).

Hosea 12:10-14. Apparently, some persons in Israel opposed prophets and even ridiculed them (Hosea 9:7-9). One purpose of this speech is to affirm that prophetic authority comes from God. Even Moses is identified as a prophet (v. 13). Verse 12 contains another reference to Jacob.

Hosea 13:4-16. This announcement of punishment begins with a paraphrase of the first lines of the Ten Commandments (Exodus 20:2-3). In a single verse, God reminds Israel of the Exodus, the covenant, and the Law.

Hosea 14:1-8. This section has some of the appearance of liturgy. The prophet calls for Israel to return to God (vv. 1-2a). He instructs the people in the words of a prayer of penitence (vv. 2b-3). In verses 4-8, God answers the prayer with an announcement of salvation.

Hosea 14:9. This verse appears to be a later scribal addition to the book. Its point of view is similar to that of the Book of Proverbs. The pious scribe recommends the Book of Hosea to all those who are wise and would learn "the ways of the LORD."

DIMENSION THREE:
WHAT DOES THE BIBLE MEAN TO ME?

Judgment or Salvation?

What will God do with the wayward people? Is the question resolved in the Book of Hosea? If so, how? Clearly the book contains announcements of both judgment and salvation, and certainly more of the former. We may resolve the question of the relationship between good news and bad news in the prophetic book in the following ways:

Some earlier commentators proposed that the original message of Hosea consisted entirely of indictments and announcements of judgment. They suggest that the hopeful passages were added later. Few today find that solution persuasive or acceptable, although some parts of the book probably did come from later hands, for example, 14:9.

Some suggest that the positive and negative announcements come from different stages in the prophet's life and ministry. Each speech was addressed to a specific time and to specific circumstances. Circumstances determined what should be said. However, that interpretation still leaves us with the question concerning God's last word. Will God finally act to punish or to save?

Possibly the relationship between judgment and salvation is chronological. First God will punish Israel, and then act to save and restore the remnant that is left. While this view is entirely possible, and in fact is a common Old Testament viewpoint, it is never stated explicitly in the Book of Hosea.

Another possibility is that judgment applies to some of the people and salvation to others. In the case of Hosea, that interpretation is not likely. The announcements of disaster, as well as the promises of salvation, usually apply to the people as a whole.

At some points, the purpose of divine judgment seems to be to teach Israel by depriving the people of such things as idols and the institutions of kingship and cult. When this goal is accomplished, they will learn once again to rely entirely upon God.

The most distinctive answer in the book, and one that represents Hosea's distinctive understanding of God, appears in Hosea 11, especially verses 8-9. The question of wrath or mercy is on God's very heart. God struggles with the matter, knowing that the people deserve punishment. But God goes beyond human standards and even beyond the covenant. Compassion wins over anger. At least according to this passage, the last word is mercy, comparable to the good news of the New Testament. Israel has not earned that compassion. It comes solely from the divine initiative.

Given such prophetic texts, and given the New Testament understanding of God's love, where in the Christian faith is there room for a view of divine judgment in history?

What, after all, does judgment mean in the Book of Hosea and to us? The term evokes images of a divine judge. This judge weighs evidence in the light of a code of law, and hands out sentences. Such a picture easily lends itself to legalism, to trying to please a God who will always keep score. While that image applies to some of the speeches in the Book of Hosea, it does not account for all the words of the prophet. Sometimes, a legal notion of judgment does not help us understand the future or present disaster. This kind of disaster does not have to be imposed as punishment. Instead, it is brought upon people by their actions. To "reap the whirlwind" is not divine punishment; it is the inevitable result when people "sow the wind" (Hosea 8:7). Actions have their consequences, and evil actions entail evil consequences.

Paul continued to struggle with the question of judgment and salvation, law and gospel. The law continues to speak so that "the whole world [will be] held accountable to God." But no one will be justified by works of the law (Romans 3:19-20). Hosea knows that human beings cannot redeem themselves. Hosea also is convinced that God, in grace, will take the initiative to save the people.

Close today's session by listing on a markerboard or large paper any insights the group members have gained from their study of Hosea 7–14.

Your sons and your daughters will prophesy, / your old men will dream dreams, / your young men will see visions. (2:28)

THE DAY OF THE LORD IS NEAR

Joel 1–3

DIMENSION ONE: WHAT DOES THE BIBLE SAY?

Answer these questions by reading Joel 1

1. How is the Book of Joel introduced and defined? (1:1)

   The book is introduced as the word of the Lord that came to Joel, the son of Pethuel.

2. What insects have attacked the land and its crops? (1:4)

   The locust swarm has attacked the land.

3. How is the nation that has invaded the land described? (1:6)

   This nation is described as powerful and without number, with teeth like the lion and fangs like the lioness.

4. Why does Joel call for the people to mourn? (1:8-10)

   Joel calls for the people to mourn because the offerings are cut off from the house of the Lord; the priests mourn; the fields, ground, grain, wine, and oil are lost.

5. Why are the priests called to put on sackcloth and mourn? (1:13)

   They should mourn because the grain offering and drink offerings are withheld from the house of God.

6. What should the priests and the people do? (1:14)

They should declare a fast, call a sacred assembly, summon all the inhabitants of the land to the house of the Lord, and cry out to the Lord.

7. What will the day of the Lord be like? (1:15-16)

On the day of the Lord there will be destruction from the Almighty. Food, as well as joy and gladness, will be cut off.

Answer these questions by reading Joel 2

8. What will happen when the day of the Lord is coming? (2:1)

The trumpet will be blown, the alarm sounded, and the people called to tremble because the day of the Lord is coming and is near.

9. How does the prophet describe the enemy? (2:4-5)

The enemy appears like the galloping along of war horses, rumbling like chariots, like a fire consuming the stubble, and like a mighty army drawn up for battle.

10. Whose army is it that causes the earth to shake and the sun and moon to be darkened? (2:10-11)

The Lord's army causes the earth to shake and the sun and moon to be darkened.

11. What does the Lord want the people to do? (2:12-13)

The Lord wants the people to return with fasting, weeping, and mourning and to rend their hearts and not their garments.

12. Why should the people return to their God? (2:13-14)

God is gracious and compassionate, slow to anger, and abounding in love. God might turn and have pity, leaving a blessing.

13. Who should come to the sacred assembly? (2:16)

All the people should come to the fast, the sacred assembly.

14. Why do the priests think God should spare the people? (2:17)

God's inheritance should not become an object of scorn, so that the people may say "Where is their God?"

15. What does the Lord say to the land, the wild animals, and the people of Zion? (2:21-23)

The Lord tells the land, the wild animals, and the people of Zion to not be afraid, to be glad, for the Lord has done great things.

16. What is the great army that the Lord had sent among the people? (2:25)

The great army is the swarming locusts.

17. What are the people to know? (2:27)

The people are to know that the Lord is their God, and that the people shall never again be shamed.

18. What are the results when the Lord's Spirit is poured out on all people? (2:28-29)

When the Lord's Spirit is poured out on all people, sons and daughters will prophesy, old men will dream dreams, and young men will see visions.

19. What are the wonders in the heavens and on the earth? (2:30-31)

The wonders are blood and fire and billows of smoke, the sun turned to darkness and the moon to blood.

Answer these questions by reading Joel 3

20. What does the Lord promise to do to Judah and Jerusalem? (3:1-2)

The Lord promises to restore the fortunes of Judah and Jerusalem, to gather the nations in the Valley of Jehoshaphat, and to enter into judgment against them there.

21. What is the Lord's accusation against Tyre, Sidon, and all the regions of Philistia? (3:5-6)

The Lord accuses Tyre, Sidon, and Philistia of taking God's silver and gold and other treasures into their temples, and of selling Judah and Jerusalem to the Greeks.

22. When war is proclaimed among the nations, what are the people to do? (3:10)

When war is proclaimed among the nations, the people are to beat their plowshares into swords and their pruning hooks into spears. The weak are to say, "I am strong."

23. What is the day of the Lord near? (3:14)

The day of the Lord is near in the valley of decision.

24. What is to happen to Egypt and Edom? Judah and Jerusalem? (3:19-20)

Egypt shall be desolate and Edom a desert waste. Judah and Jerusalem shall be inhabited forever.

DIMENSION TWO: WHAT DOES THE BIBLE MEAN?

Introduction to Joel. The Book of Joel is a report of a two-part prophetic liturgy. The first part (Joel 1:2–2:17) includes the prophet's commands to the community to convene a service of complaint and petition to God. The people are to do this because of the threat of a plague of locusts (1:4-20) and because of the danger of the day of the Lord.

The second part of the book (Joel 2:18–3:21) reports God's responses to genuine repentance. God promises salvation as a result of repentance. God assures the people that they have been heard. The danger from the locusts has evoked the fear of a cosmic day of the Lord. In the end, this day will be turned into a day of salvation, because the people have trusted in the compassion of their God.

Date and Circumstances. Knowing the date and historical circumstances of the Israelite prophets is important. Their words have been evoked by specific problems of their times. When they originally spoke the word of God, they addressed it to particular people in individual situations. Consequently, the more we know about their times, the better we can understand their words. However, knowing for certain when every prophet was active or when every book was written is not possible.

Joel is such a case. The first verse of the book, unlike that of many others, does not date the prophet in the times of Israelite or Judean kings. The book contains few clear allusions to historical events that would help us with a date. However, the contents of the book assume certain circumstances that strongly suggest that the prophet was active in the decades before or after 400 BC.

The book has no references to the Babylonian Exile or to the Babylonian or Assyrian Empires. This omission suggests that they are long past. The book contains no evidence of external unrest, such as would have come after the middle of the fourth century BC, with the rise of Alexander the Great. The political situation fits the Persian period. Furthermore, the prophet takes for granted the existence of the Temple in Jerusalem, rebuilt after the Exile, and a thriving, well-organized religious community. The leaders appear to be priests and elders, not kings or princes. Also supporting a relatively late date are the numerous quotations from earlier prophets such as Amos, Isaiah, Malachi, and Obadiah.

As we read through the books of the twelve Minor Prophets, we jump around in history. Joel probably was placed between the eighth century prophets Hosea and Amos, not for chronological reasons, but because of its similarities to Amos. Joel 3:16 parallels Amos 1:2, and Joel 3:18 parallels Amos 9:13. Both books refer to Tyre, Philistia, and Edom.

Prophets and the Cult. The evidence for Joel's institutional and religious context is clear. In fact, the prophet and the book reflect the practices of worship in the Temple very strongly. Many have argued that Joel was a "cultic prophet," that is, an official participant in the religious services.

That may appear to be a strange claim. Protestants tend to take for granted a strong contrast or even conflict between the inspired prophetic word and ritualized religion. After all, Amos was expelled from Israel by the high priest Amaziah after Amos prophesied Amaziah's death (Amos 7:10-17). Speaking for God, Amos says, "I hate, I despise your religious festivals; / your assemblies are a stench to me" (5:21). Isaiah utters similar words (Isaiah 1:10-17). Isaiah, like Amos, calls for justice and righteousness instead of sacrifices and services of worship. Hosea blames the priests (but also the prophets) for many of Israel's problems (Hosea 4:4-6; 5:1-2).

The Book of Joel reminds us that both the prophetic role and prophetic message were many and varied. The attitude of the prophets toward the official religious institutions was not one-dimensional. Most prophets participated in the religious life that they often found lacking or misguided.

Joel participated directly (probably in an official position) in Temple worship. His liturgical role was no less official than that of the priests. He gave the official call to prayer and fasting. He ordered the priests to gather the people. He gave instruction in prayer, and then proclaimed God's response to the people's genuine contrition. Furthermore, the prophet doubtless borrowed a great deal of his language from the practice of worship. Long after Joel's time, the book or parts of it were probably used in Temple and synagogue services.

Joel was no less a prophet than others such as Amos, Hosea, and Isaiah. In the last analysis, he did not speak his own words. Like all prophets, he spoke the words God revealed to him, including the revelation of future consequences.

Joel 1:4. A total economic disaster has occurred with the invasion of the locusts. The kinds of locusts listed here cannot be identified with certainty. The different kinds listed may correspond to different stages in the development of a single type. The locust plague recalls the plagues against Egypt during the Exodus. Then, the locusts ate what was left after the hail (Exodus 10:3-19).

Joel 1:5-14. The liturgical character of the book, as well as the prophet's role, is emphasized here. This section is a call to a communal complaint ceremony, well known in the rest of the Old Testament. When the community was threatened, an unscheduled prayer service was organized. The first step in the service was the summons to gather.

The call to the complaint service is organized in four parts. First, the prophet calls those who enjoy the wine to lament because of the destruction of the vineyards, as well as other plants

(vv. 5-7). Second, Joel calls upon the people to mourn like a young woman who has lost her bridegroom (vv. 8-1 0). Third, he calls for the farmers to despair for the loss of the produce of the land (vv. 11-12). Finally, the prophet tells the priests to mourn the loss of the offerings from the Temple. The priests are to gather the people to the Temple for the service (vv. 13-14). It appears that the prophet is the organizer of the worship service.

Joel 1:15-20. These verses contain the actual complaints that form the heart of the prayer service. They describe the effects of the locust plague and serve to remind God of the devastation. The prayer emphasizes that all, including the wild animals, cry to God.

Joel 2:1-2. Now Joel issues a different call to the people. This call is to sound the alarm in Jerusalem because something terrifying is about to happen. The call, including the description of the terror that evoked it, continues through verse 11. In verse 12, the prophet issues yet another and different summons to the people.

The occasion for the fearful cry is the coming "day of the LORD" (v. 1). This day is known in both earlier and later biblical traditions. The expression appears five times in Joel. In the first three occurrences (1:15; 2:1, 11), the day is against Israel. In the final two cases, it is a day against the foreign nations (Joel 2:31; 3:14).

The idea of the day of the Lord as a future event comes from the ancient traditions of the holy war. In the books of Joshua and Judges, God fought with Israel against its enemies. So the day of the Lord came to be viewed as a day of hope. But Amos saw the day as something to fear: Woe to you who long / for the day of the LORD! / Why do you long for the day of the LORD? / That day will be darkness, not light (Amos 5:18).

The day has become fearful to Amos, as in the first three uses in Joel. While God will indeed arise to destroy the enemies, the enemies of God are now the people of Israel.

Joel 2:3-11. These verses continue with a description of the terrible events on the day of the Lord. The prophet describes the invasion of the land and then even the city of Jerusalem by a ruthless and relentless army (v. 5). The soldiers move forward in battle array, and leave in their wake nothing but destruction. In fact, the effects of the invasion are cosmic. The earth shakes. The heavens tremble. The sun, the moon, and the stars all are darkened (v. 10).

Commentators have disagreed about the identity of this invading army. Some consider it a metaphorical description of the locust plague already reported or of another plague of locusts. But this is a vision of the end time, the final day of the Lord. The troops are the army of the Lord (v. 11) or some foreign army called to bring God's judgment. The cosmic dimensions of the invasion make it clear that no ordinary disaster is on the horizon. Joel has taken the appearance of the locusts as a sign that the final destruction is near.

Joel 2:12-17. These verses form the center and heart of the Book of Joel. Up to this point, an economic disaster has been described as the occasion for a call to prayer. The disaster is the sign that the final day of the Lord is near. After this section, the Lord will announce through the prophet the good news of God's intervention to save the people. The key to the change from dire and fearful circumstances to good news is contained here. These verses are, first, a call to sincere repentance, and then, the proclamation of a service of worship.

For Joel, then, God's decision for judgment or salvation hangs upon the response of the people. Will they acknowledge their sin and repent, or not? Judging from the remainder of the book, they did respond to Joel's passionate plea. But there is no report of that response in the book itself. Clearly the Book of Joel is only one side of the religious drama, the words of the prophetic leader. The actions and words of the other participants are not reported. Second Chronicles 20:1-29 reports a service of prayer when the people faced danger. It may be seen as a model of the liturgical event in the Book of Joel.

Joel 2:12-14. These verses are a call to repentance. They include the instructions for the cultic actions and words to be used by the people. Ritual and a sincere change of heart are compatible with one another. The call to "rend your heart / and not your garments" indicates that the ritual must be genuine. The word that characterizes repentance is *return*, which is used frequently in the Old Testament with such a meaning (see Deuteronomy 30:10; 1 Samuel 7:3). The verb refers to the orientation of a person's whole being toward God. It assumes that the person has in some way departed from a path of total obedience and faithfulness and has now returned fully to God.

Joel 2:13-14. The motivation for the call to turn is found in the nature of God. In the first place, God is "gracious and compassionate, / slow to anger, and abounding in love." In the second place, the people are reminded that God also is capable of repenting. Even if God promises that punishment will come, God may "turn" and "relent." That astounding belief is consistent with the understanding of God in the New Testament. God has not determined in advance what will transpire in history. History, whether it will turn out good or bad, is the result of interaction between God and human beings. Human repentance can turn judgment into salvation, because God is willing to repent.

Joel 2:15-17. This section parallels Joel 1:5-15, especially 1:14. The people are called to a service of lamentation and repentance. The prophet acts as liturgical director. He even gives the priests their instructions.

Joel 2:18-32. This section begins to report God's response to repentance by announcing the good news. Most of the words are direct quotations of the Lord. They must have been pronounced by the prophet in the context of worship. They are not unlike the point in Christian worship following the congregation's confession of sin when the minister or priest gives words of assurance or pronounces absolution.

Joel 2:21-27. The good news is a reversal of the disaster that begins this prophetic book and a promise that the day of the Lord will not come. Words of reassurance are announced, even to nature itself (vv. 21-22), and then to the people. Former conditions will be restored.

Joel 2:28-32. Throughout the Old Testament, God's "Spirit" gives life and power to human beings. Here, however, Joel has a special gift of the Spirit in mind. The people will become a nation of prophets. The context emphasizes that the people will "know" that God is in their midst and there is no other God (2:27). The emphasis is upon the close and immediate relationship between God and people. Through the gift of the Spirit, all the people will see and know God's will, as do prophets with whom God communicates through dreams and visions.

Joel 3:1-8. These verses return to ancient themes concerning the day of the Lord, understood as a holy war against the enemies of Israel. The nations will be called to account for their injustice against Israel. The enemies, and especially the Philistines, will receive what they have given others.

Joel 3:9-15. The themes of holy war against the enemies of God's people, and thus enemies of God, continue with a call to battle. The prophet certainly knew of the promise of eternal peace found in Isaiah 2:4 and Micah 4:3, and has reversed it. Joel has not completely contradicted the promise of peace. He has already announced good news to Israel. He has, however, modified the older prophetic vision in a significant way. Isaiah and Micah saw all nations coming peacefully to Jerusalem to learn God's law. Joel calls for a final day of war against the nations and then peace for Israel.

Joel 3:16-21. This section, which stresses the centrality of Jerusalem and its Temple, employs traditions found in the Book of Amos. Joel 3:16a depends upon Amos 1:2; Joel 3:18 borrows from Amos 9:13. The fruits of nature will be boundless, the enemies put to shame, and Israel will dwell secure forever. These events will happen because "the LORD dwells in Zion" (v. 21)!

DIMENSION THREE:
WHAT DOES THE BIBLE MEAN TO ME?

The Day of the Lord

You may wish to initiate the discussion by asking the group members to say what the expression "day of the LORD" means to them. Joel reflects both earlier and later views of that day as the time when God will come to change history. The day will be one of divine warfare against God's enemies. In some cases, the enemy is seen as the people of Israel; in others, as the foreign nations. In either case, God is expected to act to establish justice. In the Bible, then, the "day of the LORD" evokes both fear and hope.

Similar fears and hopes are expressed even more dramatically in the Book of Revelation. Revelation contains a vision of the end of history. First will be a terrible day of judgment, especially against those who oppose the people of God (see Revelation 14:14-20; 19:17-19.) But then there will be "a new heaven and a new earth" and a "new Jerusalem, coming down out of heaven from God" (Revelation 21:1-2). Tears, death, mourning, crying, and pain will be no more.

The place of the foreign nations, or of those who oppose the people of God, poses special problems for reflection on such fears and hopes. The Old Testament has more than one perspective on that question. Joel sees death and destruction for the enemies. Other prophets look to the salvation of all nations. This issue can be focused by contrasting Joel 3:9-10 with Isaiah 2:1-4 and Micah 4:1-4. As we have seen, Joel has turned the vision of peace into one of war. How can we account for the different hopes? Can we reconcile the two with one another, that is, hold both at the same time? If not, which view is right for you? How should the message of Jesus concerning the kingdom of God affect our reading of these passages?

The Relationship of Repentance to Salvation

Most often in the Old Testament, as in Joel, the salvation of the people of God is expected in history and on the earth. People will have plenty to eat. They will live in peace. They will know the presence of God among them. Our Christian faith tends to think of salvation as spiritual, and the kingdom of God as beyond history. How do passages, such as Joel 2:18-19, with their emphasis on material things, fit with our Christian understandings? Perhaps Joel reminds us of those other New Testament emphases in this regard. Those who encountered Jesus began, in their lifetimes, to experience the kingdom of God. That concern for the material well-being of others embodies the will of God.

The turning point in the Book of Joel, and the transformation of fear into hope, takes place as soon as the prophet calls for genuine repentance (Joel 2:12-17). We must presume, by the words of reassurance that follow, that the congregation did as Joel asked. This change from judgment to salvation is not unlike that in the Book of Jonah. In Jonah, the people of Nineveh sincerely repented, and God spared them. Repentance and prayer are often individual and personal matters, however, Joel speaks of communal worship and a service of repentance led by the priests. He does not reject ritual. Instead, he emphasizes that the words must reflect the deepest commitment of the worshipers to change. They must direct their lives once again toward God.

What is to come in the future is a free act of God, but always in interaction with others in community. No magical words will determine what is to be. The God of the Bible is willing and able to be affected by human actions and words. And the very foundation of the act of repentance here is the people's trust in God's compassion and their faith in the eventual triumph of that compassionate God.

Conclude the session by asking group members what insights they have gained from the study of the Book of Joel. List questions the book has raised for them.

You only have I chosen / of all the families of the earth; / therefore I will punish you / for all your sins. (3:2)

THE LORD ROARS FROM ZION

Amos 1–4

DIMENSION ONE: WHAT DOES THE BIBLE SAY?

Answer these questions by reading Amos 1

1. When did Amos see his words concerning Israel? (1:1)

    Amos saw his words in the days of Uzziah, king of Judah and Jeroboam, son of Jehoash, king of Israel, two years before the earthquake.

2. What happens when the Lord roars from Zion and thunders from Jerusalem? (1:2)

    When the Lord roars, the pastures of the shepherds dry up and the top of Carmel withers.

3. Why does the Lord refuse to revoke the punishment of Damascus? (1:3)

    The Lord refuses to revoke the punishment because they have threshed Gilead with sledges having iron teeth.

4. What will happen when the Lord breaks down the gate of Damascus, and destroys the king of the Valley of Aven and the one who holds the scepter from Beth Eden? (1:5)

    When these things happen, the people of Aram will go into exile to Kir.

5. Why will the Lord send fire to destroy the walls and fortresses of Gaza? (1:6-7)

    Fire will destroy the walls and fortresses of Gaza because they took captive whole communities into exile to Edom.

6. What are the sins of Tyre? (1:9)

> *Tyre sold whole communities of captives to Edom and disregarded a treaty of brotherhood.*

7. Why does the Lord refuse to revoke the punishment of the Ammonites? (1:13)

> *The Lord refuses because they ripped open pregnant women in Gilead in order to extend their borders.*

Answer these questions by reading Amos 2

8. Why does the Lord refuse to revoke the punishment of Judah? (2:4)

> *The Lord refuses because they have rejected the law of God and failed to keep God's decrees, and their false gods have led them astray.*

9. How does Israel treat the righteous, the needy, the poor, and the oppressed? (2:6-7)

> *Israel sells the righteous for silver and the needy for a pair of sandals. They trample the poor and deny justice to the oppressed.*

10. What does Israel do in the house of God? (2:8)

> *In the house of God, Israel drinks the wine taken as fines.*

11. What has the Lord done for the people of Israel? (2:9-11)

> *God completely destroyed the Amorites, brought Israel out of Egypt, led her in the desert for forty years, gave her the land, raised up some of her sons to be prophets and some of her young men to be Nazirites.*

12. What are the people of Israel accused of doing to the Nazirites and the prophets? (2:12)

> *The people are accused of making the Nazirites drink wine and commanding the prophets not to prophesy.*

13. When the Lord judges Israel, what will happen to the swift, the strong, and the warrior? (2:14)

> *The swift will not escape, the strong will not muster their strength, and the warrior will not save his life.*

Answer these questions by reading Amos 3

14. Why will the Lord punish Israel for all its sins? (3:2)

    The Lord will punish Israel because they are the only people, of all the families of the earth, whom God has chosen.

15. What does the Lord do without revealing the divine plan to the prophets? (3:7)

    The Lord does nothing without revealing the divine plan to the prophets.

16. What is happening in Samaria? (3:9-10)

    There is great unrest and oppression; people do not know how to do right; persons hoard plunder and loot in their fortresses in the mountains of Samaria.

17. What houses does the Lord promise to destroy on the day of Israel's punishment? (3:15)

    God promises to tear down the winter house, the summer house, houses of ivory, and the mansions on the day of Israel's punishment.

Answer these questions by reading Amos 4

18. What does the Lord swear to do to the women called "cows of Bashan"? (4:1-3)

    Because they oppress the poor and call for their husbands to bring them something to drink, God swears that they will be taken away with hooks and fishhooks, taken out through breaks in the wall, and cast out toward Harmon.

19. What do the people of Israel love to do when they come to Bethel and Gilgal? (4:4-5)

    They love to sin and sin yet more, to bring their sacrifices and tithes, to give a thank offering, and to brag about freewill offerings.

20. What is the refrain that recurs five times in Amos 4:6-11?

    The refrain is "'yet you have not returned to me,' / declares the LORD."

21. What did the Lord withhold when there were just three months before the harvest? (4:7)

    God withheld the rain when there were just three months left before the harvest.

22. When the Lord overthrew some, as when Sodom and Gomorrah were overthrown, what was Israel like? (4:11)

When the Lord overthrew some, as when Sodom and Gomorrah were overthrown, Israel was like a burning stick snatched from the fire.

23. What does the Lord call for Israel to do? (4:12)

The Lord calls for Israel to prepare to meet God.

24. Who forms the mountains and creates the wind? (4:13)

The Lord God Almighty forms the mountains, creates the wind, reveals God's thoughts to human beings, turns dawn to darkness, and treads on the heights of the earth.

DIMENSION TWO: WHAT DOES THE BIBLE MEAN?

Introduction to Amos. The Book of Amos contains mostly short, prophetic speeches. It also contains reports of the prophet's visions, the account of one event in the prophet's life, and three short hymns or fragments of hymns (Amos 4:13; 5:8-9; 9:5-6). The book has two major sections. Chapters 1–6 contain speeches. Chapters 7–9 are organized around five vision reports. Chapters 1–4, the focus of this lesson, begin with the superscription and motto of the book (1:1-2). Next, they offer a series of prophecies against foreign nations (1:3–2:5), then culminate in prophecies against Israel (2:6–4:13). The message of the prophet is clear and strong. Because of their social injustice and religious arrogance, God will punish the people of Israel with a total military disaster.

Date and Circumstances. Amos contains sufficient evidence for determining the date and some of the circumstances of the prophet. The superscription (1:1) places Amos in the reigns of two kings, Uzziah of Judah (783–742 BC) and Jeroboam II of Israel (786–746 BC). References elsewhere in the book, especially 7:9-10, confirm this report. These verses also verify that the prophet was a native of the South who came to the North, Israel, to proclaim the word of God. While the earthquake (1:1) cannot be identified, the report that the prophet spoke "two years before the earthquake" suggests that Amos was active for a short time, certainly less than a year.

Historical allusions and the circumstances assumed by the prophet place him in the last decade or so of Jeroboam II. This date would be about 760 BC. The reigns of Jeroboam II and Uzziah were long and relatively peaceful. There had been no significant threats from major powers such as Egypt or Assyria. The peace seems to have led to prosperity, at least for a few. According to Amos, this prosperity was gained at the expense of many. There seems to have been a breakdown in the old tribal and family systems of land ownership. A wealthy group was emerging at the top of the society.

But Israel and Judah would not be left on their own much longer. At about the time that the long reigns of Uzziah and Jeroboam ended, a new and aggressive king came to the throne in Assyria. He was Tiglath-Pileser III (745–727 BC). He set out to incorporate the little states of Syria and Palestine into his empire by military force. He did not live to conquer Israel, but his successors invaded the Northern Kingdom. They destroyed its cities and carried the people into exile. Samaria, the capital city, fell to Sargon II in 722/21 BC, and the history of Israel came to an end. Thus the prophecies of Amos were fulfilled some forty years after he uttered them.

Few details are preserved concerning the life of Amos. His home of Tekoa is in the Judean hills south of Bethlehem. He was a shepherd, who also cared for sycamore-fig trees by trade (7:14), and was called to prophesy in Israel. For the most part, *Israel* in the book refers to the Northern Kingdom in contrast to Judah. *Israel* does not usually mean the nation as a whole. Amos addresses his words particularly to those who live in Samaria, the capital, and in Bethel, the location of a major sanctuary.

The Book. While Amos is the earliest prophet whose words are preserved in a book, speaking of him as a "writing prophet" is misleading. He was a speaker. His addresses were short and memorable. They consisted mainly of accusations and proclamations of punishment. Some of his speeches were reports of threatening visions. Possibly, Amos later dictated his speeches to someone. He even could have written them down himself. But it is more likely that the addresses were collected and recorded by others. Those who put the speeches together seem to have been close to the prophet and agreed with what he said. They may have been his disciples.

Not everything in the book would have been spoken by Amos. The first verse of the book looks back on the prophet's activity and talks about him. Also the story of the prophet's clash with Amaziah the priest of Bethel (7:10-17) speaks of Amos from the perspective of a third party. A few other passages reflect a different and later perspective. They must have been added as the book was saved and circulated in Judah. These passages include the prophecy against Judah (2:4-5), the hymnic passages (4:13; 5:8-9; 9:5-6), the concluding prophecies of hope (9:8b-15), and a few others.

The preservation of the book and the additions to it are testimony that the words of the prophet, while originally uttered for one particular time and place, continued to be heard by later generations as the word of God.

Traditions and Theology. The words of Amos are so startling and dramatic that they might appear to be unprecedented. But the message of the prophet did not arise out of thin air. Rather, Amos repeatedly assumes or appeals to traditions that he and his hearers held in common. Among these is the belief that God brought Israel out of Egypt and granted the people the land of Canaan (2:9-10; 3:1-2; 9:7-8). The prophet also takes it for granted that the people have always known what God expected of them. Consequently, he is not introducing any new moral or legal expectations. He is simply holding them accountable for their transgressions. Israel had known from the beginning that God expects justice and righteousness. In this respect Amos is not radical, but conservative. He calls Israel back to what had been revealed from the beginning of its history. Nor is the announcement of judgment because of such sins an innovation.

Amos builds upon earlier beliefs and traditions, but he does introduce some new developments. He seems to have been the first to stress that Israel's election itself may be the reason for judgment (3:1-2). Israel is not the only people God has chosen (9:7-8). Amos also seems to have been the first to announce total and complete judgment upon Israel. He proclaims that God is about to bring the history of Israel to an end.

Amos 1:2. When God roars through the voice of the prophet, the results may be devastating. Amos and other prophets believed that the word of God through the prophets is understood to be powerful and effective. This word is not merely urging what should be done or warning what may happen, but setting events into motion (see also Jeremiah 1:10).

Amos 1:3–2:16. These seven prophecies against foreign nations conclude with a prophecy against Israel. They are almost monotonous in their repetition of the same formulas. All begin with the formula, "This is what the LORD says." Most conclude with "says the [Sovereign] LORD." Each speech introduces the crimes of the particular nation. The introductory phrase is, "for three sins of . . . / even for four, I will not relent." The numerical formula suggests an indefinite number. Another way for this phrase to be translated is, "for crime after crime." Each time, one or more violations are listed, followed by the announcement of punishment through fire, destruction, and often exile.

As noted in the participant book, the emphasis falls upon the last speech, the prophecy against Israel. The addresses against the other nations are no less serious though. The foreign nations are held accountable for generally accepted principles of fair and humane behavior toward their neighbors. Judah, a foreign nation to Israel, is accused of violating the revealed law of God. Israel's sins are listed in specific detail. They have dealt unjustly with the poor (2:6-8). They have failed to appreciate God's saving acts on their behalf (2:9-11). And they have acted against those chosen to do God's will (2:12).

Amos 3:1-2. This speech is filled with irony, as frequently happens in Amos. The most valuable gift that God has given Israel has become the reason for judgment; God has established higher expectations for the chosen people. The translation of the concluding line as "therefore I will punish you / for all your sins" is somewhat misleading. The word for *punish* does not appear in the original Hebrew text. This phrase could be translated "therefore I will visit your sins upon you."

Amos 3:3-8. The sayings that begin this speech (vv. 3-6) are similar to those found in the Book of Proverbs. In each case, the prophet appeals to generally known phenomena to make the point that every effect has a cause. The principle is applied to prophecy (v. 8) to show that one speaks as a prophet because God has spoken. Especially since Amos encountered opposition to his right to prophesy (see 7:10-17), this section appears to speak against those who oppose his right to speak as he does.

Amos 3:9-11. This prophecy of punishment is against Samaria, the capital city of Israel. The sins are stated broadly, including "unrest," "oppression," and "plunder." However, the punishment that God has in store for them is described concretely. They will suffer an invasion by an enemy that will break down the fortifications and plunder. Those who live by violence shall die by violence.

Amos 3:12. Again, the prophet's words are ironic. Later prophets such as Isaiah speak hopefully of a remnant that will survive the coming destruction. Amos describes those who will be left as the "two leg bones or a piece of an ear" that the shepherd snatches from the hungry lion, or as those "with only the head of a bed / and a piece of fabric from a couch" (see Amos 5:3).

Amos 3:13-15. Two kinds of buildings are singled out for destruction when Israel is punished. The altars of Bethel and the fine houses of the wealthy will be destroyed. Amos brings together here the two reasons he sees for Israel's coming demise. Israel shows religious arrogance, represented by their pride in the great sanctuary at Bethel. They also have failed to achieve justice and righteousness; it is implied that the wealthy have built their mansions at the expense of the poor.

Amos 4:1-3. These verses contain a typical prophetic speech, which was probably delivered as a single address in Samaria. The speech begins with a call to attention, addressed to the wealthy women of the capital city (v. 1a). The rest of the first verse describes the women in terms of their sinful behavior. They are lazy, arrogant, and have oppressed the poor and needy. The prophet moves from an indictment to an announcement of punishment. He asserts that God has sworn what is about to happen to the women. Verses 2 and 3 describe the brutal treatment of captives after a city has been defeated by an enemy. The "breaches" (v. 3) are the breaks made in the city walls when the enemy breaks through. The gruesome image of captives carried off with hooks is not just a figment of the prophet's imagination, but corresponds to scenes in Assyrian bas-reliefs of their victories.

Amos 4:4-5. Important sanctuaries were located at Bethel and Gilgal (see Genesis 28:10-22; Joshua 5:2-9; Amos 7:10-17). The prophet speaks as if he were a priest or other worship leader addressing pilgrims on their way to Bethel or Gilgal. But what comes out is a parody of the pilgrim song or call to worship. This speech serves, in effect, as an indictment of the people, for whom *worship* and *transgression* have become synonymous. Amos does not explain here how or why that is the case. In a similar criticism of worship elsewhere (5:21-24), he calls for justice and righteousness instead of offerings and services of worship.

Amos 4:6-12. This section contains a series of units linked by the concluding refrain, "'yet you have not returned to me,' / declares the LORD." The passage interprets disasters such as famine, drought, and military defeat as God's means of motivating the people to repent. But these attempts have failed, and Israel is called to "meet" God. The prophet surely does not have in view a pleasant encounter.

Amos 4:13. This hymn fragment or doxology, like the others in Amos (5:8-9; 9:5-6), probably was not spoken or written by the prophet himself. This verse was possibly a later addition to the book. It likely comes from the time of the Babylonian Exile (after 597 BC). This addition shows that the words of Amos were taken seriously and used in community worship long after the prophet had left the scene. The Judeans of the Exile believed and accepted what the Israelites in the time of Amos rejected: the sins of the people lead to disaster.

DIMENSION THREE:
WHAT DOES THE BIBLE MEAN TO ME?

The Meaning of Election

The election of the people of Israel as God's chosen is taken for granted by both Amos and those he addressed. But the prophet has brought a new perspective on this ancient conviction. He reminds the people that election entails special responsibilities and dangers. He also points out that God has cared for and will hold accountable other peoples as well.

Some of the early religious leaders in America believed that this new territory was like a new Jerusalem and its citizens were, like Israel, God's own chosen people. This notion still has its adherents. Does Amos challenge us to reconsider and broaden our beliefs in election just as he challenged those people of ancient Israel? Keep in mind that the prophet did not deny that God elects people in special ways. He saw the implications of election, and he knew that God was free to elect others as well.

Often in the sayings of Jesus and in other New Testament passages, the question of Israel's election is considered. Ask the group members if they can think of examples (include Matthew 15:21-28; Luke 15; Acts 7, 10:7-38; Romans 3:9-26).

God's Judgment

The words of Amos pose for us one of the most troubling themes of the Old Testament. The prophet proclaims that God is about to destroy the nation of Israel because of its sins. There is no easy way around this view. It is tempting to consider the prophet's words as threats; their purpose, however, is to bring about repentance through warning the people of the consequences of sin. In three or four brief cases (5:4-7, 14-15, 21-24) repentance is emphasized. Elsewhere, and almost without relief, the prophet announces what God is about to do. He states the future destruction as a fact resulting from human sin.

Invite the group to consider the relationship between God's wrath, justice, and love. Recognize that the New Testament is the last word for Christians, and that the first Christians affirmed that the God revealed in Jesus is the God of ancient Israel. Then ask the group to consider how the message of Amos should be heard.

Is it true that human experience often confirms the view that evil behavior leads to bad consequences? Are there exceptions to this rule, especially in the suffering of the righteous? Should we then take human suffering to be the will of God?

You may wish to conclude the session by asking the members of the group to list and record what they have learned from this study of Amos 1–4, and what questions the biblical text has posed for them.

But let justice roll on like a river, / righteousness like a never-failing stream! (5:24)

JUSTICE AND RIGHTEOUSNESS

Amos 5–9

DIMENSION ONE:
WHAT DOES THE BIBLE SAY?

Answer these questions by reading Amos 5

1. How does Amos identify the "word"? (5:1)

   Amos identifies the "word" that he takes up concerning Israel as a "lament."

2. What will happen to the city that marches out a thousand and the city that marches out a hundred? (5:3)

   The city that marches out a thousand shall return with only a hundred; the city that marches out a hundred shall return with only ten.

3. What does the Lord call for Israel to do? (5:4-5)

   The Lord calls for Israel to seek God and live, and not to seek Bethel or go to Gilgal or journey to Beersheba.

4. Whose sins are great? (5:12)

   Those who oppress the righteous, who take bribes, and who deprive the poor of justice in the courts have great sins.

5. What will the day of the Lord be like? (5:18-20)

   "That day will be darkness, not light. / It will be as though a man fled from a lion / only to meet a bear, / as though he entered his house / and rested his hand on the wall / only to have a snake bite him."

6. How does the Lord feel about Israel's feasts, assemblies, offerings, and songs? (5:21-23)

The Lord despises Israel's feasts and religious assemblies, refuses to accept all kinds of offerings, and refuses to listen to Israel's songs.

7. What does God want to happen instead of feasts? (5:24)

God wants justice to roll on like a river and righteousness like a never-failing stream.

Answer these questions by reading Amos 6

8. To whom does Amos address his cry of woe? (6:1)

Amos addresses his cry to those who are complacent in Zion and to those who feel secure on Mount Samaria.

9. What is to happen to those who live in luxury? (6:4-7)

Those who live lives of luxury but "do not grieve over the ruin of Joseph" will be among the first of those to go into exile.

10. What have the people done to justice and the fruit of righteousness? (6:12)

The people have turned justice into poison and the fruit of righteousness into bitterness.

Answer these questions by reading Amos 7

11. What did Amos do after his vision of locusts eating up the crops? (7:1-3)

Amos prayed that God forgive Jacob because it could not survive the destruction, and God relented.

12. What did God do after Amos's vision of judgment by fire? (7:4-6)

After Amos's vision of judgment by fire, Amos prayed that God forgive Jacob because it could not survive the destruction, and the Lord again relented.

13. How does the Lord explain the meaning of the vision of the plumb line to the prophet? (7:7-9)

The plumb line indicates that God will spare them no longer, that the high places of Isaac and the sanctuaries of Israel will be ruined. God will rise against the house of Jeroboam with the sword.

14. Of what does Amaziah accuse Amos? (7:10-11)

   Amaziah accuses Amos of conspiring against the king, for he has said Jeroboam will die by the sword, and Israel must go into exile.

15. Why does Amaziah prohibit Amos from prophesying at Bethel? (7:13)

   Amaziah tells Amos not to prophesy at Bethel because it is the king's sanctuary and the temple of the kingdom.

16. Why does Amos speak against Israel? (7:14-15)

   He speaks against Israel because the Lord took him from tending the flock and told him to go prophesy to the people of Israel.

17. Why will Amaziah and his family be punished? (7:16-17)

   Amaziah and his family will be punished because he has told Amos not to prophesy against Israel and not to preach against the house of Isaac.

Answer these questions by reading Amos 8

18. What vision is the occasion for announcing that the end has come upon the people of Israel? (8:1-3)

   A vision of a basket of ripe fruit is the occasion for announcing that the end has come upon the people of Israel.

19. What do those say, who trample the needy and do away with the poor of the land? (8:4-6)

   They ask when the New Moon will be over that they may sell grain; when the sabbath be ended that they may sell wheat, cheat persons, buy the poor and the needy, and sell refuse ("sweepings") with the wheat.

20. What will the Lord do "in that day"? (8:9-10)

   On that day God will make the sun go down at noon. God will darken the earth in broad daylight, turn religious feasts into mourning, and turn songs into weeping.

21. What kind of famine will there be in the days ahead? (8:11-12)

    There will be a famine, not of food or water, but of hearing the words of the Lord.

Answer these questions by reading Amos 9

22. Who will escape the judgment of the Lord? (9:1)

    The Lord will decapitate those who are left when the pillars are destroyed, and no one will escape the judgment of the Lord.

23. What will the Lord do to those who hide at the bottom of the sea? (9:3)

    The Lord will command the serpent to bite those who hide from God at the bottom of the sea.

24. In addition to bringing Israel up from Egypt, who else did the Lord bring up, and from where? (9:7)

    The Lord also brought up the Philistine from Caphtor and the Arameans from Kir.

25. What will happen to all the sinners among God's people? (9:10)

    All the sinners among God's people who say, "Disaster will not overtake or meet us," will die by the sword.

26. What will the Lord do to David's fallen shelter? (9:11)

    The Lord will raise up David's fallen shelter, repair its broken places, restore its ruins, and rebuild it.

27. What does the Lord promise to do concerning the fortunes of the people of Israel? (9:14)

    The Lord promises to restore the fortunes of the people of Israel.

DIMENSION TWO: WHAT DOES THE BIBLE MEAN?

Background. Chapters 5–9 include the last part of the collection of prophetic speeches. These chapters also include the entire second section of traditions organized around the five vision reports. Between the third and fourth vision reports is the story of a conflict between Amos and Amaziah, the priest of Bethel (7:10-17). The visions, like virtually all the speeches of Amos, announce that God is about to intervene in history. God will judge the nation of Israel through a total military defeat because of Israel's sins, especially social injustice and religious arrogance.

The Composition of the Book. In the previous lesson, we observed that Amos did not write the book that bears his name. The prophet was not an author in anything like the modern sense. Rather, he was a speaker who, in the name of God, addressed with short speeches all those who would listen. The present book is a collection of those addresses. Moreover, some material in the book does not go back to the ministry of the original prophet. These were added as later generations applied the words of Amos to their own times.

The vision reports in Amos 7–9 provide some insight into the growth and composition of the book. Considered by themselves, these five reports present an ordered sequence. They are all similar in some respects. They begin with a formula that designates what follows as a vision ("This is what the Sovereign LORD showed me"). Then they report what was seen, and give the meaning. All but the last include some dialogue between the prophet and God. The first two (7:1-3, 4-6) are parallel to each other. They are visions of threatening things (locusts, fire). The prophet responds by interceding on behalf of the threatened people, and God repents of the planned judgment. The next pair (7:7-9; 8:1-3) are also parallels. The visions (plumb line and basket of ripe fruit) are not themselves threatening objects. But these objects become the basis for announcements of judgment. The prophet does not intercede. The final vision report (9:1-4) is distinctive in both form and content, consistent with its placement as the final word. This vision is of God standing over the altar, commanding that it be destroyed. None of the people will escape judgment.

Viewed by themselves, therefore, the vision reports are a consistent and logical presentation. They lead from the threat of punishment, at first withheld when the prophet intercedes, to stronger and stronger announcements of total disaster.

But the vision reports do not stand alone in the present form of the book. Rather, other traditions interrupt the sequence. The story of the encounter between Amos and Amaziah (7:10-17) stands between the third and fourth vision reports. Why? The only logic to this placement seems to be the principle of *catchwords* in collecting oral or written traditions. The first verse of the story (7:10) contains the name *Jeroboam*, which also occurs in the last verse of the third vision report (v. 9). The catchword served as a mnemonic and linking device, connecting traditions that were originally independent.

In all likelihood, the five vision reports once were handed down as a distinct block of the Amos tradition. The other material, including both the story and the speeches in Amos 7–9, were added later. Amos 1–6 might have been formed as a collection of the prophet's speeches before they were included with the vision reports. The process of developing the book from short, oral addresses would have been complicated. The process must have included many faithful people. Some of those may have heard Amos speak. Others were probably from subsequent generations who knew that the words of the prophet were the word of God.

Amos 5:1-2. Following the call for Israel to "Hear this word," the prophet sings a funeral song. He even uses the poetic meter and tone for such expressions of grief. The one who has died is the virgin Israel. The prophet's dirge is an announcement of punishment on Israel. The prophets freely used forms of speech from all spheres of Israelite life to present their messages in forceful ways. As elsewhere, Amos employs irony.

Amos 5:3. This verse may be a continuation of the dirge. It may have originally been uttered on a different occasion. In any case, the message stresses how many will die, not how many will be left.

Amos 5:4-7. The word *seek* here probably is a technical term for inquiring of God or turning to God in a service of prayer. *Seeking* the Lord is contrasted with *seeking* Bethel, *going* to Gilgal, and *journeying* to Beersheba. Bethel and Gilgal were known to be major centers of worship.

Amos 5:8-9. Like two other texts in the book (4:13; 9:5-6) these lines appear to be part of a hymn of praise or a doxology. Hymns such as this were known in the time of Amos. The doxologies were probably added to the book much later, when the words of Amos were being used in Israelite worship. In any case, the lines are powerful. They celebrate God as both the Creator of the cosmos and the One who can act to change the course of history.

Amos 5:10-13. The rich and powerful are accused of depriving the poor, the righteous, and the needy of their rights. The expression "in court" ("in the gate" in the NRSV) indicates that Amos is particularly concerned with the corruption of the law courts. In ancient Israel, both civil and criminal trials were conducted in the gateway of the city. The gateway served as a public gathering place. At least in early times, individuals presented their complaints "in the gate" before the elders who gathered there. To hate the one who "upholds justice in court" is to refuse to listen to one who tells the truth. To "take bribes" and "to deprive the poor of justice" is to corrupt the courts, especially at the expense of those who cannot defend themselves.

Amos 5:14-15. Along with verses 4-7 and 21-24, these lines are the only pleas in the book in which the prophet states in positive terms what is expected of the people. The only specific meaning to doing good here is the call to "maintain justice in the courts" of law.

Amos 5:18-20. Following the cry of "woe," Amos accuses the people of false expectations concerning the day of the Lord. He emphasizes that the day will be the opposite of what is expected. Both the prophet and his audience are aware of an ancient tradition concerning the day of the Lord. According to that tradition, the day was the time when God would come to fight against the enemies of Israel. According to Amos, God will indeed appear to fight enemies. But the enemies are now the people of Israel.

Amos 5:21-27. Compare this address with Isaiah 1:10-17. In both cases, the prophets imitate the practice of the priests responding to inquiries from the laity concerning proper sacrifices. In the voice of God, they reject all religious observances. They call instead for the practice of justice and righteousness. Isaiah appears to say that unjust behavior makes a person unworthy to come before God. Amos appears to reject all religious practices in favor of how persons should behave toward others in society.

Amos 6:1-7. Like other prophets, Amos frequently began his addresses with the cry, "woe." What usually follows is a description of the wrong behavior of those addressed. The prophet directs these two "woe" speeches to the wealthy and powerful. In the first case (vv. 1-3), he criticizes their self-satisfaction. He accuses them of ignoring the dangerous signs of the times. In the second case (vv. 4-7), he paints a picture of the idle rich who are not concerned about "the ruin of Joseph." The leaders of revelry will be the leaders into exile.

Amos 6:8-14. This section on the destruction of Israel is not a single, unified prophetic speech. It includes diverse materials and various styles of expression. Verse 8 has God swearing a solemn oath to "deliver up the city," doubtless to its enemies. Verses 9 and 10 present a mysterious little scene of survivors hiding among the ruins and the bodies of the slain. Verses 12 and 13 use proverbial sayings ("Do horses run on the rocky crags? / Does one plow the sea with oxen?"). These sayings show that Israel's sins are unnatural behavior. Verse 14 is another speech by the Lord, promising that God will bring an enemy to oppress the people from one end of the land to the other.

Amos 7:1-9. Three of the five vision reports in the book occur here. The others are in 8:1-3 and 9:1-4. With the exception of the last one, all begin with "This is what the Sovereign LORD showed me" or "I saw the LORD . . . and he said." This is a standard formula for introducing such accounts. Likewise, all but the final vision in 7:1-9 involve dialogue between the prophet and God. In the first two accounts, Amos prays for the people. These prayers indicate that prophets did more than communicate the word of God to the people. They could also intercede with God on behalf of the people. Moreover, ancient Israel knew that God was capable of responding to prayer, even to the point of "relenting" of the evil God planned to do.

Locusts (v. 1) were a familiar threat to crops and, therefore, to the lives of the people. The "judgment by fire" (v. 4) is no ordinary flame but one that will destroy both the earth and the waters believed to surround the heavens and the earth (see Genesis 1:2).

Amos 7:10-17. The story of the conflict between Amos and the priest of Bethel is reported from the perspective of a third party. At stake is the question of the prophet's authority to speak in Israel. Amos was a citizen of Judah. The words of Amos could not be simply ignored, for they were believed to be powerful. Consequently, Amaziah, the priest of Bethel, sent a message to King Jeroboam, charging Amos with conspiracy against the state (vv. 10-11).

Amaziah confronted the prophet. Without repeating the accusation of conspiracy, he told him that Amos had no authority to prophesy at Bethel. Amos must return to his own country (vv. 12-13). By telling Amos to earn bread in Judah, the priest implies that Amos is earning money as a prophet. Amos denies that he is the kind of prophet Amaziah seems to assume he is. Amos insists that he prophesies simply because God compelled him to do so. Amos pronounces judgment upon the priest, his family, and his people (vv. 7:14-17). The basic accusation against Amaziah is that he has tried to stand in the way of the word of God.

In some ways, this story presents the conflict between institutionalized religion and the solitary, inspired prophet. But one should not exaggerate that contrast. On the one hand, the institutions, the government, and the priesthood had always viewed themselves as established by the same God who called Amos. On the other hand, though, Amos was an individual. Amos and the role he filled did not spring from thin air, but had a long history. Many prophets preceded Amos. He had learned from their tradition how to not only hear the word of God but also speak it. Prophets, including Amos, were part of an "institution" no less than priests and kings. The conflict is between institutions more than between institutionalized religion and the solitary individual. Moreover, Amos was not alone. There was at least one supporter or disciple who passed on the report of the argument.

Amos 8:1-3. This fourth vision report announces judgment upon Israel. The vision itself is simply the basis for a play on words. The Hebrew term for ripe fruit (*qayits*) sounds like the word for end (*qets*). The end is described as a time of death and mourning.

Amos 8:4-10. Several short speeches continue to accuse the people of their eagerness to cheat the poor and the needy (vv. 4-6). Verses 7-8 announce that God has sworn to make the land tremble. The people will have a day of mourning (vv. 9-10).

Amos 8:11-14. God will punish Israel by depriving the people of the word of God. Those who swear by the false gods of Samaria, Dan, and Beersheba receive special condemnation.

Amos 9:1-4. This final vision report is a fitting climax to the series, and to the message of the prophet as a whole. Its form is unlike the others. Before, the prophet described visions involving natural phenomena. But here, the prophet reports that he had a vision of God beside or over the altar. God was commanding total judgment: "Not one will get away, / none will escape" (v. 1).

Amos 9:7-8. While Amos does not preach universalism, he does broaden Israel's horizons. The people had come to view their election by God arrogantly. Amos points out that God had been concerned for and had brought up other nations as well. Those other peoples, to be sure, would not have acknowledged that they were led by God. But that refusal does not change the opinion of Amos. Israel's election has become the occasion for the self-satisfaction on the part of the people. Therefore, they will be judged.

Amos 9:9-15. Most of these lines were not written by Amos. They were added much later by those who read and believed what the prophet had said. These are words of salvation in a book that announces total judgment. The vocabulary also belongs to a later age and historical perspective. These sentences assume that the speakers and audience are in the midst of the ruins of the judgment and the Exile. Though the lines probably are not from Amos, they are no less important and authoritative. Those who experienced the judgment announced by Amos now see God acting to save and restore.

DIMENSION THREE:
WHAT DOES THE BIBLE MEAN TO ME?

Amos 5:10-15, 21-24; 8:4-6—Justice and Righteousness

Ask the group members to think about the various contemporary uses and misuses of the word *justice*. When and where is this word most commonly used in our society? The term occurs in a great many contexts. Most frequently and precisely it occurs in relation to the courts, state and federal legislatures, and the system of laws. Amos, likewise, understands the term, in large measure, in relation to the judicial system of his time. He charges that justice is being corrupted. Ask group members to consider some contemporary parallels to these ancient violations of the rule of justice. Amos was convinced that the poor and the weak were not getting fair treatment in the courts. In what situations does that also happen today?

Whatever else it means, "to do justice" means to do what is fair. The exact meaning of justice in any given situation often is difficult to establish. That is why civil suits come before the courts. One party may believe that he or she has been done an injustice, and that the other party must make it right. The other party claims that there is no injustice. One purpose of the laws and the courts, then, is to define *justice*. They do so, in part, by establishing procedures by which justice can be determined.

If the purpose of a legal system is to maintain justice, what role does or should the church play in such matters? Amos obviously did not hesitate to tell his hearers that they were abusing their legal system, and that some persons were being denied justice. Amos also saw that justice was intimately related to righteousness, a quality of life that leads people to deal fairly with others. The prophet also seems to have had no difficulty seeing the difference between justice and injustice. Amos had such insight for two reasons. First, the laws and legal procedures had been established long before his time. He considered them just. Second, he believed the laws given to establish justice to be expressions of the nature and will of a just and righteous God.

Amos 7:10-17—Prophets and the State

The story of the conflict between Amos and Amaziah shows us the relation between religious and political authority. Our society and that of Amos are different. Church and state were not separated in ancient Israel. The differences between the prophet and the priest may then be understood as a confrontation between the politically established religious authority and what Amos claims is the word of God.

Certainly, the goals of religious faith and of government coincide at many points. The purpose of the legal system, as discussed above, may be one such point. Both church and state are committed to establishing justice, maintaining peace, and protecting the weak from the strong. Ask group members to consider this question: Are there situations in which it is difficult to "give back to Caesar what is Caesar's, and to God what is God's" (Matthew 22:21; Mark 12:17) at the same time? Ask the group to think of such cases. The prophet Amos and the Bible as a whole leave no doubt that, when such conflict arises, our first loyalty is to God.

You may wish to conclude the session by asking the group members to list the insights they have gained from their study of Amos 5–9.

See, I will make you small among the nations. (Obadiah 2)

GOD'S PEOPLE AMONG THE NATIONS

Obadiah 1-21 and Jonah 1–4

DIMENSION ONE: WHAT DOES THE BIBLE SAY?

Answer these questions by reading Obadiah

1. Which nation does Obadiah's vision concern? (v. 1)

     Obadiah's vision concerns the nation of Edom.

2. What does the Lord plan to do to Edom? (v. 2)

     The Lord plans to make Edom small among the nations and utterly despised.

3. Why does the Lord announce disaster for Edom, so that shame will cover it? (v. 10)

     God announces disaster for Edom because of the violence it has done against Judah ("your brother Jacob").

4. What should Edom not have done? (v. 12)

     Edom should not have looked down on Jacob in the day of misfortune, rejoiced over the people of Judah in the day of their destruction, or boasted in the day of trouble.

5. What will happen to all the nations on the day of the Lord? (vv. 15-16)

     On the day of the Lord, their deeds will return on their heads, they will drink continually, and they will be as if they had never been.

6. What will the houses of Jacob, Joseph, and Esau be? (v. 18)

   The house of Jacob will be a fire, the house of Joseph a flame, and the house of Esau stubble. Jacob and Joseph will burn and consume Esau.

7. Who will go up to Mount Zion and govern the mountains of Esau? (v. 21)

   Deliverers will go up to Mount Zion and to the mountains of Esau. The kingdom will be the Lord's.

Answer these questions by reading Jonah 1

8. Where does the Lord command Jonah to go; what is he to do, and why? (1:2)

   Jonah is to go to Nineveh and to preach against it because the wickedness of the people has come to God's attention.

9. Why does Jonah go to Joppa and board a ship to Tarshish? (1:3)

   Jonah goes to Joppa and boards a ship to Tarshish in order to run away from the presence of God.

10. What do the sailors do when the storm threatens to break up the ship? (1:5)

    Each of the sailors cries to his god, and they throw the cargo into the sea to lighten the ship.

11. Why are the sailors afraid when Jonah tells them who he is? (1:10)

    The sailors are afraid when Jonah tells them who he is because they know he is running away from God.

12. What do the sailors do to Jonah? (1:12-16)

    They cry to the Lord to save them and forgive them, and then, at Jonah's request, they throw him into the sea.

13. How long is Jonah inside the fish? (1:17)

    Jonah is in the fish for three days and three nights.

Answer these questions by reading Jonah 2

14. What does Jonah say the Lord did for him? (2:5-6)

    When the waters engulfed him, God brought up his life from the pit.

15. What does the fish do when the Lord speaks to it? (2:10)

    The fish vomits out Jonah onto dry land.

Answer these questions by reading Jonah 3

16. What does Jonah do when God speaks to him again? (3:1-3)

    Jonah obeys and goes to Nineveh.

17. What does Jonah proclaim as he goes through Nineveh? (3:4)

    As he goes through Nineveh, Jonah proclaims that in forty days Nineveh will be overthrown.

18. What does the king of Nineveh do when he hears the news? (3:6-8)

    The king of Nineveh rises from his throne, removes his robe, covers himself with sackcloth, and sits in dust. He also publishes a proclamation calling all citizens and all animals to observe a fast, cover themselves with sackcloth, call to God, and give up their evil ways.

19. Why does the king of Nineveh send the proclamation? (3:9)

    He sends the proclamation so that God may yet relent, turn from fierce anger, and they may not perish.

20. What does God do after seeing that the people of Nineveh have turned from their evil ways? (3:10)

    God has compassion and does not bring upon the people the destruction God had threatened.

Answer these questions by reading Jonah 4

21. How does Jonah respond to God's decision not to destroy Nineveh? (4:1)

    Jonah was greatly displeased and angry with God's decision not to destroy Nineveh.

22. What does Jonah do, and why? (4:5)

    Jonah goes out of the city, makes a shelter for himself, and sits in its shade in order to see what will happen to the city.

23. What is the Lord's final word to the angry prophet? (4:11)

    The Lord's final word to the angry prophet is a rhetorical question, "Should I not have concern for the great city of Nineveh?"

DIMENSION TWO: WHAT DOES THE BIBLE MEAN?

This lesson covers two very different books. Obadiah, the shortest book in the Old Testament, is a series of prophecies concerning God's reign. Its central theme is that God will punish the enemies of Israel. Israel's ancient adversary and neighbor Edom will be especially punished. The Book of Jonah is unique among the prophetic literature. This is not a collection of the addresses of a prophet. Jonah tells the story of a reluctant prophet who becomes bitter when God does not destroy Nineveh. Both books, then, address the same issue, the relationship of the people of God to foreign nations. But their answers are radically different. Obadiah calls for revenge. Jonah calls for understanding and acceptance.

Introduction to Obadiah. The book contains little direct information about the prophet and the historical circumstances in which he worked. Commentators have not been able to agree on the specific date or situation that brought forth this book. Verses 11-14, in particular, describe Edom's participation in the destruction of Jerusalem by the Babylonians in 587 BC. Was Obadiah an eyewitness, or is he making use of a tradition that had been handed down for decades or even centuries? Verses 6-9 describe the destruction of Edom. This destruction actually took place between 500 and 450 BC. Were those lines written before the fact as prophecy, or after the fact? The concluding verses (17-21) announce the return from the Babylonian Exile and the restoration of the nation. Was this passage written in advance or after the fact? The book probably was written either late in the Exile or soon after the return (ca 550-510 BC). But it also incorporates traditions that are as old as 587 BC.

Possibly, the book was composed for use in worship. The prophetic proclamation of punishment upon Israel's enemies and salvation for the people of God doubtless was part of services in both the first and second Temples. Moreover, the book has similarities to certain psalms. The book is especially like those that celebrate the enthronement of the Lord (Psalms 47; 93; 96). The concluding verse of the book announces the coming reign of the Lord.

To understand this book, one must appreciate the situation of the people of Judah during the Exile and in the years after their return. The political, economic, and religious crises were monumental. They had lost their independence as a nation. They had been reduced to slavery.

Their Temple was destroyed. All this had occurred at the hands of their neighbors, including Edom. Did these events mean that the God of Israel was not in control of history, that the promises of the covenant were ended? Was there no justice in the world?

In many ways, the Book of Obadiah is one answer to some of these questions. That answer is similar to the answer given in Psalm 137. The psalm presents the agony of the Exile. It then calls for the punishment of those who brought the agony about. Obadiah affirms that there is justice, the justice of retribution (see v. 15). Moreover, the book affirms that the Lord is still the God of history and the One whose reign will be established over the world (v. 21). The fall of Jerusalem to the Babylonians and their gods raised questions about God's power. Obadiah reaffirms that the Lord is God of the world and of history. The day of the Lord will redress the wrongs and restore the people.

If these are positive points, then the negative must be noted as well. Justice as retribution is not the only, or the deepest, understanding of justice in the Old Testament. The vision of the reign of God in the book is narrow, suggesting the exclusion of all nations but Israel.

Obadiah 1-4. Some of these verses closely parallel Jeremiah 49:15-16. Obadiah seems to have borrowed the language from Jeremiah to set the theme and tone of the book.

Obadiah 5-10. Verses 5-6 appear to depend upon Jeremiah 49:9-10. Edom faces, or will face, a political and military crisis. Its allies and friends are turning against it. Leadership will be lost, and eventually Edom will be totally destroyed.

Obadiah 11-14, 15b. Determining the accuracy of these details about the participation of Edom in the destruction of Jerusalem is not possible. However, 2 Kings 25:3-7 reports that, when a breach was made in the wall, King Zedekiah and "the whole army" fled to the South. That is in the direction of Edom. But they were not able to escape.

Obadiah 15a, 16. With these verses, the perspective of the book is broadened. The judgment now encompasses all nations and all of history. The day of the Lord is approaching when God will exercise authority over the world.

Obadiah 17-21. The restoration foreseen here will involve not just Jerusalem and Judah. All of the ancient empire of Israel will be restored. The borders will expand to include the territory that had been taken by Edom, among others. The center of God's reign will be Mount Zion in Jerusalem.

Introduction to Jonah. The Book of Jonah stands out among the other prophetic books because it is a story *about* a prophet instead of a collection of prophetic speeches. It also stands out because it is in prose instead of poetry. The book does contain poetry, but it is a hymn instead of an oracle. The book is a single narrative of the call of a prophet. It tells of his eventual obedience to that call, what happened along the way, and what happened after the prophet had done what God told him to do.

Questions and even debate usually arise among readers of the book concerning its historical reliability. Did all these events occur as the account says they did? The evidence, including comparison of this narrative with others in the Bible, leads some commentators to conclude that the book is not intended to report actual events. They feel that the book conveys a message, that it is neither prophetic biography nor history, but a work of inspired imagination. In this sense, the book is like the parables of Jesus. In parables, the truth is in the message, instead of the accuracy of history.

Consequently, the question for modern readers in the church is not whether or not a "great fish" swallowed Jonah during the time of the Assyrian Empire. The question is much more difficult. Can we accept the writer's claim that all people are children of God? Can we accept the subtle insistence that God has a message for all people?

Jonah is similar to several other books and parts of books. Ruth shares its acceptance of the role of foreigners in God's world. But Jonah is also similar to Esther, which does not accept foreigners. It shares with the Wisdom Literature the interest in literary care and in the human characters. Its point of view is prophetic, though. It criticizes narrow parochialism. The book calls for the word of God to those outside the community of faith.

Nothing is known about the author of the book. The date and circumstances can be fixed only in very broad terms. The setting of the account is the time of the Assyrian Empire, which fell in 612 BC. By the time of the writing, Nineveh had become a legendary city. The book was written no earlier than the end of the Babylonian Exile in 538 BC and no later than about 250 BC, when the prophetic canon was completed. After the return from the Exile, several religious parties or groups developed. Each vied for control of the main institutions, including the Temple, the priesthood, and the government. During most of the period, those in control saw little or no place for non-Israelites in Judaism. But some persons disagreed. The main issues in the Book of Jonah were actively debated more than once during those centuries. The author was inspired to write the book sometime during the postexilic period to counter the claim of some contemporaries that faith in the God of Israel meant the rejection of foreigners.

The author of Jonah was a literary artist. This fact is revealed in the structure of the book. While it presents a single story with a clear plot, the book is composed in two distinct and parallel parts. Part one includes chapters 1–2. Part two includes chapters 3–4. Each part has three scenes that parallel the scenes in the other part. God's commission and the prophet's response in part one (1:1-3) parallel the commission and response in part two (3:1-4). The account of the storm, the pious pagan sailors, and their conversion to the God of Israel in part one (1:4-16) parallel the report of the repentance of Nineveh in part two (3:5-10). The account of Jonah's prayer in the belly of the fish in part one (1:17–2:10) parallels both his prayer and God's response in part two (4:1-11).

Perhaps even more powerful than the symmetry and balance of the stories is the skillful treatment of the characters. Only a few characters appear, but each is sketched memorably. You may wish to ask the members of the group to identify and describe the main characters and say which ones they identified with as they read the story.

Jonah 1:1-3. The lines that begin the book are not unlike those found in other prophetic books or stories of prophets. They report a revelation to a specific individual, calling him to speak God's word. The first indication that this story will be different occurs when Jonah fails to do as he was told. The account of the northern king Jeroboam II alludes to a prophet named "Jonah son of Amittai" (2 Kings 14:25). Nineveh was the capital of the Assyrian Empire until it fell in 612 BC. The location of Tarshish is not known for sure. Judging by the story, we would expect the city to be at the other end of the world from Nineveh. It probably was in present-day Spain, at the far end of the Mediterranean from Joppa, which was on the coast of Palestine.

Jonah 1:4-17. The focus in this scene is upon the contrast between Jonah and the pagan sailors. The sailors are presented in a favorable light. The conclusion of this stage of the story comes when the sailors "greatly feared the LORD" (v. 16). This change anticipates the later repentance of all the people of Nineveh. Everything is seen as working toward that goal. When God "sent a great wind on the sea" (v. 4), the purpose was to get Jonah headed in the right direction. In the meantime, the storm, along with Jonah's confession of faith (v. 9), leads to the conversion of the sailors. We also see that the power and authority of God is not limited to the land of Israel. It extends to all the world and is inescapable.

Jonah 1:7. Casting lots to find a guilty party was a common practice in ancient Israel and elsewhere (see Joshua 7:16-18; 1 Samuel 14:40-42; Acts 1:26). Such a practice, which must have originated as magic, could be used because "its every decision is from the LORD" (Proverbs 16:33).

Jonah 1:14-15. When their prayers to God bring no result, the sailors throw Jonah into the sea, at his request. The storm ceases. When we read the narrative, we think the sailors are saved because the cause of the trouble, Jonah, is no longer on their ship. But two other explanations of the effects of throwing the prophet overboard are possible. The sailors may have carried out divine justice by throwing the guilty one to his death. Or they may have done what they considered to be a sacrifice to the deity.

Jonah 1:17–2:10. Three narrative verses in this section (1:17; 2:1, 10) frame Jonah's prayer. Because the role of the "great fish" is generally misunderstood, Jonah's prayer is widely misinterpreted as a cry for help, a prayer of petition. "The LORD provided a huge fish" (1:17) to save Jonah from drowning in the sea. The prophet's prayer is a song of praise and thanksgiving for that salvation.

Like other hymns of thanksgiving in the Psalms, this one is addressed to God. The hymn includes an account of the previous distress (v. 2), which specifically identifies the trouble with the ocean (vv. 3, 5). The prophet says that, when in distress he cried to God (vv. 2, 4, 7), who heard him (vv. 2, 6). Finally, he expresses his thanksgiving and praise (v. 9) (see Psalms 18; 69; 116).

The prayer from the belly of the fish develops different themes from the narrative. The story can be read without disruption if the prayer is left out. Some commentators have suggested that the psalm was added to the book by someone other than the writer of the story. The hymn writer could have taken a hymn already in use in the Temple in Jerusalem (see allusions in vv. 4, 7) and modified it to fit the story. Because hymns and prayers are used freely in different circumstances, the same motifs occur repeatedly in the Book of Psalms.

The presence of this prayer adds depth to the Book of Jonah, addressing issues of life and death. The prayer affirms that the "God of heaven, who made the sea and the land" (Jonah 1:9) is also present and powerful when we approach death (2:5-6). The New Testament saw in Jonah, not only the sign of judgment (Matthew 16:4; Luke 11:29), but also an announcement of the resurrection of Jesus (Matthew 12:40).

Jonah 3:1-4. Given the troubles and dangers that followed his flight from his call, we are not surprised that Jonah responds obediently the second time. Jonah's message (v. 4) is the shortest, most direct form of a prophetic announcement of judgment. No indication is given that either God or the prophet called for or expected repentance. The purpose of the speech was to set the judgment into motion (see Amos 1:2). The purpose also is to make it clear to the hearers that the disaster was brought by God. Jonah's reactions confirm that he neither desired nor expected anything but judgment on the foreign city and all its inhabitants.

Jonah 3:5-10. To the original readers, the sudden and complete repentance of the people of Nineveh would have been an unexpected development. Looking back, however, we can see that the pagan sailors' confession of faith in God (1:16) should have prepared us for such a turn. Even more difficult for many modern readers to accept and understand is the climax of the entire story: God "relented and did not bring upon them the destruction he had threatened" (v. 10). But a foundational conviction in biblical faith is that the God of creation and history is also personal. God is affected by what human beings do and feel.

Jonah 4:1-11. This final conversation between God and Jonah interprets the meaning of the entire story. Jonah is like many narrow nationalists in Judaism. He is angry and offended because God did not destroy the hated city. God gently rebukes Jonah. God points out that Jonah is self-centered. Why should God not be concerned for all the human (and even animal) population of Nineveh?

DIMENSION THREE: WHAT DOES THE BIBLE MEAN TO ME?

Obadiah 20-21—The Elect and Outsiders

Old Testament texts such as Obadiah often have been embarrassing to modern Christian readers. Obadiah cries for vengeance against Edom. The book seems to embody precisely that religious parochialism and narrow nationalism criticized by the Book of Jonah. Does Obadiah have anything of value for us? It does, after all, stress the sovereign power of God, who will triumph. It does view the past and the future in terms of justice, though the understanding of justice is limited to retribution. And it does remind us of the importance of a sense of being elected by God. Israel survived the disaster of the Exile and subsequent threats because the people knew they had been chosen by God.

Jonah and the Mission of the Faithful

To Christian readers, the perspective of the Book of Jonah on this matter is consistent with the New Testament. The author of Jonah is more than tolerant and open toward foreign peoples. These foreign peoples are represented by the pagan sailors and the people of Nineveh. The writer holds up the prophet to ridicule. The prophet is more concerned about his own reputation and well-being than about such peoples. The Book of Jonah expresses a prophetic vision of God as Lord of all the world and all its peoples. God judges those who retreat to narrowness.

Ask the members of the group if they think the Book of Jonah is a prelude to the commission to make disciples of all nations. If we consider the book in that light, what may we learn from it concerning the mission of the church? If we define mission as crossing boundaries with a message, what are the boundaries for the church? What should the church's message be?

Jonah also invites us to reflect on the characteristics necessary for those who carry out God's mission. In the characterization of Jonah, the book suggests that God can use even reluctant and unattractive people to take the word across boundaries. These people can bring about dramatic and positive changes.

You may wish to conclude the group session by asking the members to list on a large sheet of paper or markerboard what they have learned from their study of the books of Obadiah and Jonah. List also what questions remain for them concerning the meaning and implications of these books.

Hear this, you leaders of the house of Jacob, / you rulers of Israel, / who despise justice. (3:9)

7

JUDGMENT ON JERUSALEM

Micah 1–3

DIMENSION ONE: WHAT DOES THE BIBLE SAY?

Answer these questions by reading Micah 1

1. When did the word of the Lord come to Micah? (1:1)

Micah "saw" a vision of the Lord about Samaria and Jerusalem during the reigns of Jotham, Ahaz, and Hezekiah, kings of Judah.

2. Who is called to hear? (1:2)

All the people, the earth, and all that is in it are called to listen.

3. What will happen when God comes forth? (1:3-4)

God will tread the high places of the earth. As a result the mountains will melt, and the valleys will split apart.

4. Why are Jacob and Israel being punished? (1:5)

The transgression of Jacob is Samaria and the sin of the house of Judah is Jerusalem.

5. What will happen to Samaria? (1:6-7)

Samaria will become a heap of rubble, a place for planting vineyards. Its foundations will be laid bare. Its images and idols will be broken, burned, and destroyed.

6. Why does God promise to weep and wail? (1:8-9)

God promises to lament and weep, go barefoot and naked, howl and moan because Samaria's wound is incurable.

7. What has come down from the Lord to the gate of Jerusalem? (1:12)

Disaster has come down from the Lord to the gate of Jerusalem.

8. Why is Lachish called to harness a team to the chariot? (1:13)

Lachish is called to harness a team to the chariot (for escape) because the transgressions of Israel were found in Lachish's people.

Answer these questions by reading Micah 2

9. What do those who plan iniquity and plot evil do at the morning's light? (2:1-2)

At morning's light, they carry out their evil. They covet fields and seize them, covet houses and take them, defraud people of their homes and their inheritance.

10. What will people say when they wail? (2:4)

The people will say they are utterly ruined. They will say that God divides the people's possession, takes it from them, and assigns their fields to traitors.

11. What do "their" prophets say to Micah? (2:6)

They say to Micah that he should not preach of "these things; / disgrace will not overtake us."

12. What kind of prophet does Micah say the people want to have? (2:11)

They want a prophet who is a liar and deceiver, saying he will prophesy for them for plenty of wine and beer.

13. What does the Lord promise to do to the remnant of Israel? (2:12)

The Lord promises to bring together the remnant of Israel like sheep in a pen.

Answer these questions by reading Micah 3

14. To whom is this chapter addressed? (3:1)

    The chapter is addressed to the leaders of Jacob and the rulers of Israel.

15. How do the evil rulers treat God's people? (3:2-3)

    The rulers' actions are comparable to eating the flesh of the people, stripping off their skin, and chopping them up like meat for the pan.

16. Why will the Lord refuse to answer the leaders? (3:4)

    God will refuse to answer the leaders because of the evil deeds they have done.

17. Of what are the prophets accused? (3:5)

    The prophets lead the people astray, proclaim "peace" when they have something to eat, and prepare to wage war against anyone who does not give them food.

18. What will happen to the seers and the diviners? (3:7)

    The seers shall be ashamed and the diviners disgraced because there is no answer from God.

19. What does Micah claim about himself? (3:8)

    Micah claims that he is filled with power, the Spirit of the Lord, and justice and might.

20. What have the rulers done? (3:9-10)

    They despise justice and distort all that is right; they build Zion with bloodshed and Jerusalem with wickedness.

21. How does Micah summarize his accusations against the leaders, the priests, and the prophets? (3:11)

    Micah accuses the leaders of taking bribes, the priests of teaching for hire, the prophets of telling fortunes for money, and all of them of claiming divine support and expecting no disaster.

DIMENSION TWO:
WHAT DOES THE BIBLE MEAN?

Introduction to Micah. The Book of Micah is a collection of prophetic speeches. It contains prophecies of both judgment and salvation. The book has two major sections, each of which has two parts. The organization of the book is thematic, moving from judgment to salvation in both major sections. The first section is Micah 1–5: chapters 1–3 consist almost entirely of prophecies of punishment; chapters 4–5 are mostly prophecies of salvation. The second section, Micah 6–7, moves again from prophecies of punishment (6:1–7:6) to prophecies of salvation (7:7-20).

Micah 1–3, with the exception of the superscription (1:1) and one prophecy of salvation (2:12-13), is a series of prophecies of punishment. They are addressed to the capital cities of the Northern and Southern Kingdoms, Samaria and Jerusalem. They include indictments of the leaders and main officials, including prophets. Because of the corruption and selfishness of their leaders, Samaria and Jerusalem will fall to their enemies.

Micah the Prophet. Most of what we know about Micah is found in the first verse of the book. He is dated in the reigns of three kings of Judah: Jotham, Ahaz, and Hezekiah. The single reference to the prophet outside the book, Jeremiah 26:18, confirms that Micah came to Jerusalem in the reign of Hezekiah. Other allusions within the Book of Micah are consistent with a date in the last part of the eighth century BC. Whether Micah was active before or only after the fall of Samaria in 721 BC is not known. Do his references to the trouble that befalls the capital of the Northern Kingdom come before or after that event?

Micah went from the small town of Moresheth to prophesy in Jerusalem. He would have been speaking at the same time that Isaiah was active. But unlike Isaiah, who was a native of Jerusalem and in frequent contact with the king and other leaders, Micah was an outsider. He was a controversial figure, evoking rejection from the populace for his words of judgment (especially 2:6-11). He must have been unpopular with the leaders he condemned (3:1-4) and the wealthy he criticized (2:1-5). He was also eager to separate himself from priests and from other prophets, whom he considered to be corrupt (3:5-8). No report of his call to be a prophet is recorded, but he was clear and firm in his conviction that he was an authentic prophet of God (3:8).

Micah's Message. The messages of Micah and Isaiah, his contemporary, have important similarities. Both prophets focused on Jerusalem, Zion, and the leadership of the nation. Micah knows the ancient tradition of the Temple on Mount Zion. He speaks of it as the Lord's place, from which God comes to judge the earth (1:2-3). But he is critical of the popular view that, because God has chosen Zion as a dwelling place, the people of Jerusalem and Judah have nothing to fear (2:6; 3:9-12). On the contrary, Micah constantly calls attention to the failure of the people. He calls attention to the leaders in particular. They have failed to act with justice. The sense of that justice comes from God. God expects justice to stand at the heart of Micah's call (3:8). No temple, however sacred, can save a people whose political and religious leaders fail to embody such divine justice. God, says Micah, will act to balance the scales. And in this case, such balancing means judgment upon the nation.

Micah 1:1. This superscription is like those that begin most of the other prophetic books. It probably was written by later disciples, who were interested in passing the words of Micah on to later generations. The verse amounts to an explanation and an interpretation of the book as a whole. It emphasizes that the words of Micah, originally spoken but now written down, are divine revelation. They are "the word of the LORD." The superscription makes it clear that these words originated in a particular time, "the reigns of Jotham, Ahaz and Hezekiah." The words concerned a specific audience, "Samaria and Jerusalem." Like the incarnation of God in Jesus of Nazareth, the words of the prophets come in particular historical times and places. To help us understand what the words of the prophets mean to us in our times, we should first learn what they meant when they were originally uttered. In this case, they were spoken in the last decades of the eighth century BC.

Micah 1:2-7. This speech begins with a call to begin a trial. In fact, it is a summons to the defendant. Next, the prophet describes the appearance of God as witness and judge (vv. 3-4). Then the indictment against the accused is read (v. 5). Finally, punishment is announced (vv. 6-7). The basic features of the speech conform to the pattern of a criminal trial. But the speech is similar to others that, perhaps, could be called the prophetic lawsuit. Some scholars think prophets even spoke such words in the Israelite services of worship. The prophets would accuse Israel of its violation of the covenant and call for judgment.

The summons is comprehensive, including all the people of the earth (v. 2). Later, the accusation is directed to Samaria and Jerusalem (v. 5). The punishment is addressed only to Samaria (vv. 6-7). The accusation, or reasons for punishment, is quite general. The sins and transgressions of the nations are identified with the cities of Samaria and Jerusalem. *Sin* means rebellion against God. *Transgression* is a failure to live up to expected norms of conduct.

The announcement of punishment is quite detailed. God will turn Samaria into a ruin. The walls and buildings will be broken down to their foundations. The site will revert to farmland (v. 6). Moreover, the city's images and idols will be destroyed. The city that became prosperous through prostitution will return to that practice (v. 8). The punishment will be a military defeat such as the one carried out by the Assyrian army in 721 BC.

The account of the arrival of God as judge (v. 3) uses language that, by the time of Micah, had become traditional (see Exodus 19:18). The appearance of God is usually reported in connection with the Temple in Jerusalem. When God appears, two things are mentioned, the actual "coming [down]" of the Lord (v. 3), and the awesome, dramatic effects of that appearance upon nature (v. 4).

Micah 1:8-16. The prophet laments and wails. He sings a funeral song over the city of Jerusalem. Finally (v. 16), he calls upon the people of Jerusalem to join in the mourning. He takes no pleasure, and expresses his grief in the awesome appearance of God to condemn and judge. The form of that expression is a traditional dirge. This song, as other funeral songs in the Old Testament (2 Samuel 1:17- 27; Amos 5:1-2), has a special poetic meter. The lines alternate between three and two beats each. He speaks of the deceased with warm affection, "the very gate of my people . . . Jerusalem" (Micah 1:9), and "Daughter Zion" (v. 13).

The prophet mourns, and calls for the people of Jerusalem to mourn. Once God has come forth to judge, the city is as good as dead. The conclusion to the dirge identifies the reason it is sung (v. 16). The people will go into exile.

The song includes a long list of cities and villages. Not all of these can be located. Most of them, including the prophet's hometown, lie southwest of Jerusalem. This territory was destroyed by the Assyrian king Sennacherib in 701 BC, during the reign of Hezekiah. Possibly Micah composed this dirge while the campaign was in progress. He saw the fall of the other Judean cities as sounding the death knell for Jerusalem.

Micah 2:1-5. The cry "woe" often begins prophetic speeches in the Old Testament. The cry is usually followed, as here (vv. 1-2), by a description of the unrighteous deeds of the addressees. In this case, that description gives the reasons for punishment announced to a particular group of people (vv. 3-5). The prophet spells out the crimes. God announces the punishment. The punishment corresponds to the crime; those who take the land of others will have their own land taken. Those who "plan iniquity" and have the power to do it are wealthy landowners. The evil that they work is coveting the fields and houses of others, and taking them. Micah, in the name of the Lord, is thus accusing the wealthy of breaking the law handed down through Moses. One of the Ten Commandments prohibited coveting the property of neighbors (Exodus 20:17; 34:24).

To understand this passage, we must recognize the meaning of the term *inheritance* (v. 2). Land and land ownership were sacred in ancient Israel. God, as owner of the earth, has allotted it by tribes and families to the people of Israel (Joshua 13–19). Moreover, those who had such an inheritance were the full and free citizens of the country. They had all the rights and responsibilities that citizenship entailed. These rights included participation in the assembly at the gate, worship, and military service. To lose one's inheritance was to lose citizenship and freedom. Thus, those who used their power to expand their estates at the expense of weaker Israelites took more than land. According to the prophets such as Micah, they were tampering with the divine economy.

Micah 2:6-11. This section is a disputation, or an argument. Actually, we have before us one side of an argument. Micah is debating with his opponents. The words of the opponents are given to us only as the prophet quotes them (vv. 6, 7). The opponents accuse Micah of being a false prophet. He reacts by accusing them of injustice and of wanting prophets and preachers who speak lies.

To be a prophet in Israel was to encounter opposition and rejection. Amos was accused of sedition. He was commanded by Amaziah, the priest of Bethel, to leave the country (Amos 7:10-17). Jeremiah found himself in trouble on more than one occasion. He was even tried for saying what he felt was the word of God (Jeremiah 26). The reasons for opposition often are the same. The prophets accuse their hearers of injustice, and announce that God is about to punish them.

Micah's opponents argue that the prophet is wrong. They have done what God expects, and God is too merciful to act in judgment. But Micah keeps pointing out their deeds of injustice. They have treated the people as an enemy. They have cheated the peaceful and the trusting. They have driven women and children from their homes, and polluted the land. His final words (v. 11) are full of irony. "If a liar and deceiver comes and says, / 'I will prophesy for you plenty of wine and beer,' / he would be just the prophet for this people!"

Micah 2:12-13. This announcement of salvation is surrounded by accusations and announcements of punishment against the wealthy and the powerful of Jerusalem. This announcement of salvation to the "remnant of Israel" stands out dramatically. These verses were probably added later, during the time of the Babylonian Exile. The content of the promise and the images are similar to those found in Isaiah. Isaiah wrote of Israel's salvation and return in peace to its homeland (see Isaiah 40:11; 43:5).

Micah 3:1-4. This prophecy of punishment has an introductory call to listen (v. 1b). Also, like other prophecies of punishment, it has two major parts. One is the indictment or reasons for punishment (vv. 1c-3). The other part is the announcement of judgment (v. 4). The imagery of the indictment is vividly harsh. The prophet accuses the heads and rulers of Israel of treating the people badly. Their actions are so bad that they are comparable to cannibalism. Determining which specific crimes are in view here is not possible. We do know that the leaders are living at the expense of the people. Micah is convinced that the leaders of the people are brutalizing those for whom they are responsible. He often affectionately calls the victims "my people" (vv. 2, 3). Those who should know and maintain justice are the most corrupt of all. From those to whom much is entrusted, much will be required. The punishment may not sound harsh to us; in the time of trouble, God will hide from them (v. 4). But to those who believe in God, it is a devastating penalty. God will abandon them to their fate, refuse to answer their prayers, and leave them godless when they finally recognize that they need God.

Micah 3:5-8. In some respects, this speech about other prophets is typical. In one respect, it is unique. A prophecy of punishment, it includes the indictment or reasons for punishment (v. 5). Then comes the announcement of judgment (vv. 6-7). What is unique is the conclusion in verse 8, a dramatic and unequivocal declaration of self-justification by the prophet about his own mission and message. This conclusion makes it obvious that the prophet is engaged in a controversy with other prophets. The issue is quite simple. The answer is not easy to discern, and the stakes are high. Who is the true prophet, the one who proclaims "peace" or the one who declares to "Jacob his transgression, / to Israel his sin"?

Micah has no doubt. The other prophets in Jerusalem are corrupt, because their word can be bought. Therefore such prophets, seers, and diviners shall be disgraced. They will be left in the dark without vision or answer. But Micah is convinced that he is filled with power and the Spirit of the Lord. This power corresponds to justice and might. The true word, at least in his time and place, is one of sin and judgment.

This issue arose at other times in ancient Israel. Jeremiah, always controversial, was challenged by another prophet, Hananiah. Jeremiah prophesied disaster while Hananiah, speaking in the name of the same Lord, prophesied peace (Jeremiah 27–28). For a while at least, Jeremiah thought that he might be wrong and Hananiah right. The word of God, since it comes through human perception, is no dogma, always the same and always known.

How are we to know who is true and who is false? That the Old Testament proposes several different ways of resolving the question shows how widespread the problem was. Among others, Jeremiah suggests that the true prophet is the one who announces disaster. The prophet of peace is the false one (Jeremiah 28:5-9). There are other suggestions, including this passage in Micah and possibly Amos 7:10-17. They suggest that professional prophets are false, and those called directly by God are true. Still other passages resolve the matter by observing that the prophets whose words come true are the real prophets.

The Book of Deuteronomy has yet another way of resolving the matter. Anyone who leads the people away from the true and uncompromising worship of God is a false prophet. That theological criterion can be applied to our own situations. Is the word of the "prophet" consistent with the heart of the faith, with what we know about God?

Micah 3:9-12. These verses are the most comprehensive of Micah's prophecies about the leaders in Jerusalem. The indictment (vv. 9-11) includes all political and religious leaders. They combine corruption and greed with a false confidence that God is on their side. Moreover, the announcement of judgment (v. 12) is not limited to the punishment of the leaders. It includes Mount Zion where the Temple stands. Once again with this announcement, we encounter the powerful notion of corporate guilt and punishment. Because of the actions of some, the entire people will suffer.

DIMENSION THREE: WHAT DOES THE BIBLE MEAN TO ME?

True and False Prophecy

Help group members recognize that the issue of true and false prophecy, a lively issue in ancient Israel, is also a modern problem. We know that Micah, along with the other prophets whose words have been preserved in the Old Testament, was obviously a true prophet of God. But not everyone who heard him accepted his claim that he was called and sent by God. Consider the question by reviewing some of the ways the Old Testament attempted to recognize true prophets.

A second step might be to discuss what it means to be a prophet today. An Old Testament prophet was one who spoke the word of God. On the basis of what he or she saw in the present and knew of the past traditions of God's activity, the prophet announced what God was about to do. Prophecy today, then, might be limited to those who announce future consequences of past and present actions. Some people think of prophets predicting the end of the world. But the meaning of the prophetic role can be viewed more broadly. The prophet might be understood as one who speaks God's word: the truth.

We are faced almost daily with distinguishing between true and false "prophets." How do we tell the difference? Do we have to use words such as "thus says the Lord" to truly speak God's truth? Suppose, for example, a scientist said that, if changes are not made in many of our practices, we will make our atmosphere so polluted that one day we cannot breathe it. Could such a person be a true prophet?

Perhaps the most important step is to test any claim of truth against the heart of our faith, as Deuteronomy suggested concerning prophets. If anyone leads us away from the central truth of the one God of the universe, that person is a false prophet. And, our Christian faith would add, true prophecy will be consistent with the revelation of God in Jesus Christ.

Conclude the group session by asking the members to list what they have learned, or questions that have emerged, from their study of Micah 1–3.

What does the LORD require of you? / To act justly and to love mercy / and to walk humbly with your God. (6:8)

GOD'S PEACEFUL REIGN
Micah 4–7

DIMENSION ONE:
WHAT DOES THE BIBLE SAY?

Answer these questions by reading Micah 4

1. What will be established as chief among the mountains and raised above the hills? (4:1)

   The "mountain of the LORD's temple will be established / as the highest of the mountains."

2. Why will the people come to the mountain? (4:1)

   The people will stream to the mountain and ask to be taught God's ways.

3. What will the people do with their swords and their spears? (4:3)

   The people will beat their swords into plowshares and their spears into pruning hooks.

4. What will God do with the lame and with the exiles? (4:6-7)

   God will assemble these persons and make them a remnant and a strong nation. God will rule over them in Mount Zion.

5. Where will the people of Jerusalem be rescued and redeemed? (4:10)

   The people of Jerusalem will be rescued and redeemed in Babylon.

6. What is Daughter Zion to do with the wealth of many peoples? (4:13)

   Daughter Zion will devote their ill-gotten gains to the Lord, who is the Lord of all the earth.

Answer these questions by reading Micah 5

7. Who is to come forth from Bethlehem Ephrathah? (5:2)

    A ruler in Israel, "whose origins are from of old, / from ancient times" is to come forth.

8. What will the ruler do? (5:4)

    The ruler will stand and shepherd his flock in the strength of the Lord and in the majesty of the name of the Lord.

9. What are the "seven shepherds" and "eight commanders" to do? (5:5-6)

    They will rule the lands of Assyria and Nimrod with the sword, and deliver the people from the Assyrians when they invade.

10. What is the remnant of Jacob to be like among the nations? (5:8)

    They are to be among the nations like a lion among the beasts of the forest, a young lion among flocks of sheep.

11. What will the Lord destroy in that day? (5:10-13)

    God will destroy their horses, chariots, cities, strongholds, witchcraft, sacred stones, idols, and Asherah poles.

Answer these questions by reading Micah 6

12. What does God call to hear the accusation against the people? (6:2)

    God calls for the mountains and the foundations of the earth to hear it.

13. What has God done for the people? (6:4-5).

    God brought them up from Egypt; redeemed them from slavery; sent Moses, Aaron, and Miriam; and protected them.

14. What does God require? (6:8)

    God requires that we act justly, love mercy, and walk humbly with God.

15. What does God ask about the ill-gotten treasures, the "short ephah" (a dry measure), and the man with dishonest scales and a bag of false weights? (6:10-11)

    God asks if it is possible to forget the ill-gotten treasures and the short ephah or to acquit the man with dishonest scales and a bag of false weights.

16. Why has the Lord begun to destroy the people? (6:13)

    The Lord has begun to destroy the people because of their sins.

17. Whose statutes and practices have the people kept? (6:16)

    The people have observed the statutes of Omri and the practices of Ahab's house.

Answer these questions by reading Micah 7

18. Who has been swept from the land? (7:2)

    The faithful have been swept from the land, and no upright persons remain.

19. What do the ruler, the judge, and the "powerful" do? (7:3)

    The ruler and the judge ask for a bribe. The "powerful dictate what they desire."

20. How do children treat their parents? (7:6)

    Children treat their parents with dishonor. A man's enemies are the members in his own household.

21. What does the prophet say he will do? (7:7)

    The prophet says he will watch in hope for the Lord, to wait for God his Savior; God will hear him.

22. What will God do for the prophet? (7:9)

    God will plead his case, uphold his cause, and bring him out into the light where he can see righteousness.

23. What will happen to the enemy? (7:10)

    The enemy will be covered with shame and trampled down underfoot like mire in the streets.

24. What will the Lord do for the people as in the days when they came out of Egypt? (7:15)

    The Lord will show them God's wonders.

25. To whom will the nations turn? (7:17)

    They will turn in fear to the Lord and be afraid because of God.

DIMENSION TWO:
WHAT DOES THE BIBLE MEAN?

Background. As noted in the previous lesson, the Book of Micah has two major sections, and each section has two parts. Each section alternates announcements of judgment with promises of salvation. The first section, Micah 1–5, contains prophecies of punishment (1–3) and announcements of salvation (4–5). The second section is chapters 6–7. It contains prophecies of punishment (6:1–7:6) and announcements of salvation (7:7-20). The chapters for this lesson include the last part of the first section and all of the second section. The most persistent theme in these chapters is God's coming peaceful reign. The people will return, and the land will be restored to them.

The structure and composition of the Book of Micah can be analyzed and understood in various ways. The outline above recognizes two major sections. However, some scholars take their clue for the outline of the book from the series of similar formulas that begin speeches. Since calls to hear occur in 1:2; 3:1; and 6:1, some see the book organized into three sections (1–2; 3–5; 6–7). In any case, the book is a collection of prophetic addresses.

These addresses probably were not delivered by Micah in the eighth century BC. Some of them bear the marks of a later age. The book in its final form is probably the composition of later editors. This situation is not at all unusual. The early prophets were not writers, but speakers. Their memorable words were saved by those who agreed with them, who believed they had to be saved for later generations. As those words were copied, others were added to them. The reasons for such additions were not to correct or even change the old prophetic messages. The persons who made the additions wanted to apply them to new situations and even new centuries. What we have to deal with, then, is not just the voice of Micah. We also have to deal with the Book of Micah as a part of our Scriptures. The prophetic voices of those later additions must be taken no less seriously than that of Micah. We must not ignore them simply because we do not know the names of their authors. Furthermore, we may understand them better if we can discover the circumstances in which they were spoken or written.

Scholars disagree about how much of the Book of Micah comes from the prophet. Some commentators argue that the eighth-century prophet was exclusively a prophet of doom. They say all hopeful expressions come from a later age. They compare, for example, the sharp contrast between the announcement of destruction upon the city of Jerusalem in Micah 3:9-12, and the beautiful vision of Jerusalem as the center of God's peaceful kingdom in Micah 4:1-4. Could the prophet who expected Zion to be a ruin also expect it to be the highest mountain on earth? It is by no means certain that Micah foresaw only doom, however. He, like Isaiah of Jerusalem, could have expected the day of salvation to come after the day of judgment.

Still, it appears that some parts of the book do not come from Micah. In some passages, the style of expression and the historical perspective reflect the Babylonian Exile or later, instead of the period of Assyrian threat when Micah lived. The style of Micah 7:1-7 is quite different from that of other sections. Micah 7:8-10 seems to assume the destruction of the nation by the Babylonians. Micah 7:11-13 speaks of rebuilding the walls of Jerusalem after the return from Exile during the Persian period. The remainder of chapter 7 (vv. 14-20) probably comes from the period of the Second Temple, when the old words of Micah would have been used in worship. The people of God continued to hear, use, and struggle with the words of Micah long after he was gone from the scene.

Theology and Traditions. The message of the Book of Micah can be summarized concisely. Because of their sins, particularly those of people in powerful places, God is about to punish the people by means of military defeat and exile. Later, those people will be brought back to their land. God will then establish perpetual peace. The prophet gives the reasons for the punishment in terms of the actions of the people. But the coming salvation is an act of God's pure grace.

Along with the announcements of God's acts to come, there is much reference to history in the Book of Micah. The prophet assumes that the people have always known what God expects of them. "He has shown you, O mortal, what is good" (6:8). The references to laws that have been violated take for granted that the law has long been revealed to the people. The book also reflects knowledge of the ancient history of salvation as preserved in the Pentateuch. Micah 6:4-5 summarizes the central event in Israel's affirmation of faith. God brought them out of Egypt, led them in the desert, and gave them the land of Canaan. In this respect, then, like both Amos and Hosea, Micah is conservative and traditional rather than radical. He calls upon his hearers to remember their ancient faith.

In addition to these traditions, the Book of Micah shares with Isaiah 1–39 an emphasis upon two other traditional articles of faith: (1) the belief that God had chosen the city of Jerusalem with the Temple on Mount Zion as a special place, and (2) the dynasty of David as the chosen means for governing the people of God. The Jerusalem- Zion tradition is present in both announcements of judgment against the city and visions of eternal peace with Zion as the center. Micah 3:11 seems to mock that belief. Some are using the belief as a basis for false confidence. But Micah 4:1-4 makes the Zion tradition the basis for future hope. The stress on the Davidic monarchy is reflected in the prophet's focus upon the responsibilities of the leaders of the nation, and in the promise of a new ruler from Bethlehem (Micah 5:1-4).

Micah 4:1-4. This prophecy of salvation, with the exception of the last verse, is almost identical to Isaiah 2:2-4. . But how are we to account for the duplication of this promise in Micah and Isaiah? Did Micah, or an editor of the book, pick up the announcement from Isaiah? Did Isaiah borrow it from Micah? Or do they both come from another, more ancient tradition? That the same announcement appears in both books is not surprising. After all, Micah and Isaiah were contemporaries. Both were active in Jerusalem, and they shared a great many perspectives.

The basis of the prophetic hope voiced here is the justice and grace of the God who has chosen Israel. All peoples come to be taught the laws of Israel. The basis for peace will be a just order, where all are obedient to the divine will. All people will be just and live in harmony with one another, because there is but one just God.

The vision is a universal one, including all peoples and nations (vv. 3-4). Its center will be the Temple of the Lord of Israel on Mount Zion in Jerusalem. All people then, are to come to the one God of the earth, the God of Israel. The transformation to the peaceful kingdom of God will be cosmic. Mount Zion, actually a very modest mountain, will be elevated as the highest of the mountains, above all the hills of the earth.

Micah 4:5. This verse stands between two prophecies of salvation. The verse is a confession of faith by the people of Israel. They are aware that they still live in a time before the fulfillment of those hopeful promises. In contrast with verses 1-4, these words express the knowledge that "the nations" still affirm faith in their individual gods. They have not yet come to Zion to be taught by the God of Jacob in order to "walk in his paths" (v. 2). In such a pluralistic context, the faithful congregation of Israel promises to "walk in the name of the LORD / our God."

Micah 4:6-8. These verses continue the theme of the previous announcements. In the first two verses, God speaks directly. God promises to call together those who have been scattered. God will make a strong nation of those who are afflicted, lame, and rejected. As in 4:1-4, the center of the reign of God will be Mount Zion. In that promise, all peoples come to Jerusalem to be taught the ways of God. In these verses, the Holy City will be the capital of a powerful kingdom. Its "former dominion" over other nations will be restored.

Micah 4:9-10. This speech is addressed to Zion, personified as a woman in labor. She is first questioned about her reasons for mourning. Then she is given commands. The final words are an announcement of salvation to a city in trouble.

The expression Daughter Zion (v. 10) is an affectionate form of address to the city of Jerusalem or the hill where the Temple stands.

Micah 4:11-13. As in many other instances, good news for Jerusalem includes bad news for the enemies of Israel. Those who have ridiculed Zion will be destroyed. The metaphor that describes the punishment of Zion's enemies refers to threshing. Zion will be like an animal that beats the grain from the stem. To "devote their ill-gotten gains to the LORD" is to fulfill the ancient ordinance of the holy war, in which all booty taken was dedicated to God.

Micah 5:1-6. Salvation will come through a messiah, the anointed one of God. The Book of Micah shares with Isaiah the expectation that God will deliver Israel through a king in the line of David. In fact, the words "when she who is in labor bears a son" (v. 3) seems to echo Isaiah 7:14, "The virgin will conceive and give birth to a son." The Gospel of Matthew speaks of the birth of Jesus as the fulfillment of the ancient promise of a messiah in the line of David. Matthew 2:5-6 quotes this passage in the report of the birth of Jesus in Bethlehem.

Micah 5:7-9. That the "remnant of Jacob" would triumph over their enemies is an expression of hope. It seems to come from a time when the people of Israel were, in fact, scattered among the nations. That would have been during the Babylonian Exile, long after Micah lived.

Micah 5:10-15. This prophetic speech announces a day of judgment. The intended audience is not clear. To whom do the *you* and *your* throughout the speech refer? If these words refer to the people of Israel, then the day of judgment is not directed against Israel. Rather, it is an occasion for purging the people of all the false supports they have depended on, including horses, chariots, fortifications, and pagan practices such as sorcery and idolatry. But the words may be directed to "the nations that have not obeyed me" (see v.15).

Micah 6:1-5. In language similar to that of the first speech in the book (ch. 1), the prophet speaks for God to bring the people into court. The initial calls (vv. 1-2) signal the beginning of a trial and the proclamation that God intends to enter into a legal dispute with Israel. We would expect accusations to follow such an introduction. Instead, God speaks in defense, asking what the wrong deeds have been. God's mighty acts on behalf of Israel are then listed (vv. 3-5). These words appear to be a defense. But they are laying the foundation for accusations and words of judgment. Israel's faithlessness will stand in stark contrast to God's faithfulness.

Micah 6:6-8. These verses continue the dialogue between God and the people in the pattern of a trial. God has initiated proceedings against them. They are heard to ask how to re-establish the broken relationship with God. Then they are given an answer. The speech has two parts: the series of questions about what God requires (vv. 6-7) and the prophetic answer (v. 8). The form of the passage borrows from a priestly liturgical pattern. When worshipers came to the Temple, they asked the priest about the appropriate offering or sacrifice. The priest then answered them (see Psalms 15; 24; Isaiah 1:10-17; Amos 5:21-24).

Few words of the Old Testament are better known than the concluding line of this section. The call to "do justice" refers to human behavior in relationship to others, the care for fairness. "To love mercy" refers to the kind of love and concern that is at the heart of the covenant between the Lord and Israel. This kindness is persistently faithful. "To walk humbly with your God," means to submit your will to the will of God. God has already "shown you" this will.

Micah 6:9-16. The language of the trial, initiated in Micah 6:1, resumes. God accuses the city of its sins and announces punishment.

Micah 7:1-7. This sad song is similar to the laments of the individual in the Book of Psalms (Psalms 12; 55). But it lacks two essential characteristics of such songs. This song is not a prayer addressed to God. It does not include a petition or cry for help in time of trouble. In some ways, the passage is similar to other prophetic addresses. It begins with the cry of woe. It speaks of the sins of the society and of the punishment for those who do evil (v. 4b). But the singer does not speak in the name of God. The singer does not address an audience. He does not announce that God is about to intervene, either. The song is best understood as a meditation on the evils of the time. It is a soliloquy. The song describes the moral decay of the larger society first (vv. 1-4). Then it describes the moral decay of the smaller society, including friends and family (vv. 5-6). The final verse (7) brings a change of tone with the singer's affirmation of confidence in God.

Micah 7:8-20. This section bears the marks of its use in ancient Israel's services of worship and celebration. The language and style of many of these lines are similar to those of Old Testament psalms. Verses 8-10 are a song of trust, similar to Psalm 23, but sung by Zion personified as a woman. Verses 11-13 include a prophetic announcement of good news to Zion. Verses 14-17 are a prayer of petition like the psalms of complaint. Verses 18-20 are a hymn of praise.

These individual elements could very well have been used in the postexilic period. They might have been used in the Second Temple as part of a liturgy celebrating God's redemption of the people. While the good news celebrated here is not as inclusive as that announced in Micah 4:1-4, its foundation is just as strong. Confidence in the future is possible because of the nature of God. God pardons iniquity, acts with compassion, and is faithful to the ancient promises (vv. 18-20).

DIMENSION THREE: WHAT DOES THE BIBLE MEAN TO ME?

Micah 6:6-8—True Religion

In these verses the prophet answers the question, "What does the LORD require of you?" In fact, the passage gives two answers. The first is a series of sacrifices and offerings. The second answer is the threefold expectation: act justly, love mercy, and walk humbly with God. Some see the passage as a total rejection of the Israelite sacrificial system. It is true that the passage contrasts with priestly and prophetic understandings of religion in the Old Testament. But this passage, as well as other similar texts (see Amos 5:21-24; Isaiah 1:10-17), rejects acts of worship and sacrifice from a people who do not act justly in their daily lives. Worship, however sincere, cannot become a substitute for lives lived in accordance with the will of God.

Moreover, it would be a mistake to relegate Micah's criticism of offerings and sacrifices to antiquity. Ask the group: Where are the parallels to such offerings and sacrifices in our religious activities, including worship, tithes, and offerings? According to the prophetic understanding of religion, all life must be faithful to a just and merciful God. Such passages as this make it difficult to make a convenient separation between what is religious and what is secular. To act with justice and kindness (or steadfast love) toward your neighbor is "to walk humbly with your God."

Micah 4:1-4—The Power of Promises

Is the hope of swords becoming plowshares realistic? Some may suggest that it is even dangerous. Note that the announcement of peace in Micah 4:1-4, while global and even cosmic, is concrete and specific. It expects God's peaceful reign to come in a specific place, Jerusalem, and at some time in human history.

What effect can such promises have on the future? Ask group members to think of what it would be like to live in a world without such hopes and promises.

Christians are called to be spokespersons of God's present and future reign. They must point out, on the one hand, where God's will is being opposed. On the other hand, they must point out signs of the kingdom of God. Where people suffer and die in war, the kingdom of God has not yet come. If we see brothers and sisters at peace with one another, the hungry fed, and the cup of cold water given to the thirsty, these are signs of the reign of God.

Conclude the session by inviting group members to list on markerboard or a large sheet of paper what they have learned from Micah 4–7. Then ask what questions have been raised by these texts.

The LORD is a jealous and avenging God; / the LORD takes vengeance and is filled with wrath.
(Nahum 1:2)

GOD'S JUSTICE AND VENGEANCE

Nahum 1–3 and Habakkuk 1–3

DIMENSION ONE: WHAT DOES THE BIBLE SAY?

Answer these questions by reading Nahum 1

1. What does the prophecy concern, and how is the Book of Nahum described? (1:1)

    The prophecy concerns Nineveh, and the Book of Nahum is "the book of the vision of Nahum the Elkoshite."

2. What is the Lord's way? (1:3)

    The Lord is slow to anger and great in power. The Lord will not leave the guilty unpunished.

3. What happens when the Lord appears? (1:5)

    The mountains quake, the hills melt, and the earth trembles.

4. What is the Lord to "those who trust in him"? (1:7)

    God is good, a refuge in the time of trouble, who cares for "those who trust in him."

5. What does God promise to do in the temple of Nineveh's gods? (1:14)

    God promises to destroy the images and idols in the temple of their gods.

Answer these questions by reading Nahum 2

6. What are people of Nineveh told to do? (2:1)

The people are told to guard the fortress, watch the roads, brace themselves, and marshal all their strength.

7. How are the chariots of the attacking army described? (2:4)

The chariots are described as storming through the streets, rushing back and forth through the squares; they look like flaming torches and dart about like lightning.

8. What is Nineveh like? (2:8)

Nineveh is like a pool whose waters drain away.

Answer these questions by reading Nahum 3

9. How does the prophet describe "the city of blood"? (3:1-3)

"The city of blood" is full of chaos: "galloping horses and jolting chariots! / Charging cavalry, / flashing weapons." The city has so many casualties that people stumble over the corpses.

10. What will those who look at Nineveh say? (3:7)

They will say that Nineveh is in ruins. They ask who will mourn, where can comforters be found?

11. What nations and peoples were Nineveh's strength and allies? (3:9)

Cush (Ethiopia) and Egypt were Nineveh's strength; Put and the Libya were allies.

12. What has happened to Nineveh's infants and nobles? (3:10)

Nineveh's little ones were dashed to pieces, lots were cast for the nobles, and the great men were put in chains.

13. Why do those who hear the news of the king of Assyria clap their hands? (3:19)

They clap their hands because there is no one who has not felt his endless cruelty.

Answer these questions by reading Habakkuk 1

14. What is the prophet's initial complaint to the Lord? (1:2-4)

The prophet complains that God does not hear when he cries for help, or save when he cries, "Violence!" God makes him look at wrongs and injustice, destruction and violence; justice never prevails.

15. What nation is God raising up, and what do they do? (1:6)

God is raising up Babylon. They sweep across the whole earth and seize dwelling places that do not belong to them.

16. What is the god of the Babylonians, the guilty people who "sweep past like the wind"? (1:11)

The god of the Babylonians is their own strength.

17. What does Habakkuk ask God? (1:13)

The prophet asks why God tolerates the treacherous, and why God is silent while the wicked swallow up those more righteous than themselves.

Answer these questions by reading Habakkuk 2

18. What does God command the prophet concerning the vision? (2:2)

God commands the prophet to write the revelation, to make it plain on tablets so that "a herald may run with it."

19. What does God say about the one whose desires are not upright and the one who is righteous? (2:4)

God says that the one whose desires are not upright is betrayed, but the righteous will live by faithfulness.

20. What is to happen to those who make their neighbors drink to the point of drunkenness? (2:15-17)

They will be filled with shame instead of glory. They will drink and be exposed, overwhelmed by the violence done to Lebanon, and terrified by the destruction of the animals.

21. What does a craftsman do when he carves an idol? (2:18-19)

    The craftsman trusts in his own creation when he carves an idol.

Answer these questions by reading Habakkuk 3

22. What does Habakkuk ask of God? (3:2)

    Habakkuk asks the Lord to renew God's work, to make it known, and to remember mercy in the midst of wrath.

23. What did God do when coming out to deliver the people? (3:13-15)

    God crushed the leader of the land of wickedness, stripping him bare. God also pierced the head of the warriors of the wicked, and trampled the sea with horses.

24. What does the prophet say he will wait patiently for? (3:16)

    He will wait patiently for "the day of calamity / to come on the nation invading us."

25. What does the prophet say he will do, though the harvest and herds fail? (3:17-18)

    The prophet says he will rejoice in the Lord, in God his Savior.

DIMENSION TWO: WHAT DOES THE BIBLE MEAN?

This lesson is about two short prophetic books, Nahum and Habakkuk. The books are similar in some ways but quite distinct in other ways. Both prophets focus upon God's punishment of the enemies of Judah, and the consequent good news for the people of God. They are quite different from the earlier prophetic books such as Amos, Hosea, and Micah. Those books prophesy judgment upon the people of Israel for their sins. Both Nahum and Habakkuk include hymns and prayers that were used on liturgical occasions. They may actually have been composed for services of prayer and worship (see Nahum 1; Habakkuk 3).

Introduction to Nahum. The distinct emphasis of the Book of Nahum is celebration of the downfall of the Assyrian Empire and the destruction of the city of Nineveh, which was destroyed in 612 BC.

Unlike most other prophetic books, Nahum does not begin with a superscription that dates the prophet. However, the information in the book and the information available to us about the history of the ancient Near East enable us to date the prophet.

Taken as a whole, the book announces the imminent demise of the great city of Nineveh. Nineveh was the center of the Assyrian Empire. The combined forces of the Babylonians and the Medes overthrew the city in 612 BC. The Book of Nahum, then, would have been composed shortly before that date. However, Assyrian power had been declining for several decades. An astute observer of international events could perhaps have foreseen Nineveh's destruction much earlier. In any case, the book was not written before 662 BC, when the Egyptian city of Thebes fell, for Nahum 3:8-9 assumes that event.

For about five hundred years, Assyria had been the dominant power in most of the Near East. Periodically, Assyria would invade and subjugate the small states in Syria and Palestine. Assyria's domination in the region ebbed and flowed, depending upon the ambition of the emperors and the power of the opposition. About a century before Nahum, the Northern Kingdom of Israel had fallen, when the city of Samaria was taken by Assyria in 721 BC. Much of the population had been carried off and dispersed across the empire. Foreigners settled on Israelite territory. Subsequently, Judah had been invaded more than once, and forced to pay tribute to Assyria. Some cities had been captured. But the city of Jerusalem, though besieged in the time of Hezekiah by Sennacherib, had been spared. Whether or not it is done intentionally, Nahum speaks for peoples all over his world when he looks forward to the fall of the city of Nineveh.

Nahum was by no means the only voice interpreting the will of God in Judah and Jerusalem during his time. He very likely was a contemporary of Jeremiah, who began his work in 626 BC. Nahum was perhaps included among those whom Jeremiah criticized as prophets who cry peace when there is no peace, and announce good news for Judah when punishment is in store. Moreover, a religious reformation took place during the period when King Josiah sponsored major changes, while throwing off the yoke of Assyria. Josiah centralized worship in Jerusalem and renewed the covenant. He also reinstated the book of law, which probably corresponds to most of the Book of Deuteronomy.

Nahum 1:1. This prophetic book is the only one specifically identified as a "book." This suggests that it was written down quite early. Except for his approximate date, all we know of Nahum is this notice that he came from the town of Elkosh. The location is unknown, because Elkosh is not mentioned anywhere else in the Old Testament. In any case, the prophet's point of view reveals a close association with the Temple in Jerusalem. Nahum was probably identified as "Nahum the Elkoshite" in Jerusalem.

Nahum 1:2-11. This hymn in praise of God is a fitting introduction to the book as a whole. It sets the stage for the detailed picture of destruction that follows. It also gives the religious and theological foundation for the celebration. What is about to take place is worthy of celebration, for it comes from the Lord who "is a jealous and avenging God" (v. 2). No enemy can stand before the Lord. The imagery for the awesome effects of God's appearance is concrete. God comes in the whirlwind and the storm. The sea dries up, the mountains quake, and the hills melt. The enemy is not identified in this passage, although verse 1 makes it clear that the enemy is Nineveh.

We probably have here only part of the original hymn. The first lines (vv. 2-8) are composed as an alphabetic acrostic, but the pattern is not completed. In alphabetic hymns or poems, successive lines or pairs of lines or verses begin with successive letters of the Hebrew alphabet.

This hymn was likely composed for a service in the Temple. It was probably used there on more than one occasion.

Nahum 1:12–2:2. Identifying a train of thought in these verses is difficult. Perhaps the text has become disordered during the copying process. Some translations, such as The Revised English Bible, attempt to solve this problem by rearranging the order of the verses. It appears that we have several sayings that originally were independent of one another. For the most part, the speeches are announcements in which the prophet quotes the words of God. Verses 12-13 apparently are addressed to Judah, promising relief from the burden of Nineveh. Verse 14 addresses Nineveh with an announcement of punishment. Verse 15 again promises salvation to Judah. Although the NIV names Nineveh as the subject of 2:1, it is unclear in the Hebrew text if this is a threat against Nineveh or a warning to Judah.

Nahum 2:3-12. This passage describes the invasion and defeat of the city of Nineveh by an unnamed army. The army moves in for the attack upon the city. We see red shields and uniforms, rushing horses, and gleaming chariots (vv. 3-4). The Assyrian officers man the walls (v. 5). But they cannot stem the tide of the attackers, who approach the palace itself (v. 6). The city is plundered and captives are carried off, mourning (vv. 7-9). The final lines (vv. 10-12) picture the scene after the defeat, with the sounds of grief in the air.

Nahum 2:13–3:7. This entire unit is a prophecy of punishment upon Nineveh. God addresses the city directly, spelling out the trouble in store for it. Nineveh is punished for two reasons. Nineveh has mistreated other nations, and the city has been a prostitute in its pagan religious practices (v. 4).

Nahum 3:8-19. The book concludes with a taunting song, in which Nahum heaps ridicule on Nineveh. Just as Thebes, though mighty, had fallen; so will Nineveh. In fact, the Assyrians themselves had taken the Egyptian city of Thebes. Nahum suggests they dashed the infants of Thebes in pieces, cast lots for its nobles, and bound its great men in chains. The prophet goes on to ridicule Nineveh. He points out that all the preparations for defense will be useless. He even heaps scorn upon the king of Assyria (vv. 18-19).

Introduction to Habakkuk. The Book of Habakkuk has two major parts. Chapters 1–2 are a dialogue between the prophet and God. Habakkuk asks why God allows the people to suffer at the hands of their enemies. Chapter 3 is a hymn celebrating God's victory over the enemies of Judah.

Unfortunately for modern readers of Habakkuk, the book gives no clear indication of the prophet's dates and history. Historical allusions are present, but they are ambiguous. Consequently, interpreters have disagreed on these questions. Some scholars even question whether the entire book comes from the same prophet. The most likely historical framework corresponds quite closely to that of Nahum. Habakkuk was probably active during the last decades of the Assyrian Empire, 625–612 BC. This conclusion is based on the reference to the rise of the Babylonians (1:6), or the Chaldeans. The "wicked" throughout the book are thought to be the Assyrians. The book, then, like Nahum, addresses the issue of God's justice in the light of the power of the wicked nation of Assyria.

The only direct information we have about Habakkuk is the note that he was a prophet (1:1). However, with indirect information, we can identify him as a prophetic visionary who was active in the Temple in Jerusalem. We are reminded once again that some prophets were active as priests in worship, probably composing hymns and liturgies.

Habakkuk 1:2–2:5. The theme of this section is quite similar to the Book of Nahum, although it is addressed differently. To the prophet, the faithful people of God are being oppressed by a wicked foreign power, probably Assyria. Whereas Nahum hears God promising to destroy Nineveh, Habakkuk struggles with God over the problem. Why do the righteous suffer? For him, the suffering is not necessarily the problem. The problem is that God's justice does not appear to operate, which is a matter of faith. He thus carries on a dialogue with God. The prophet's side of the dialogue is in the form of individual songs of complaint or lament. These are found frequently in the Book of Psalms (Psalms 5; 6; 17; and others). As in other complaint songs, the prophet bases his complaint and plea on his confidence that God is just and almighty. Will such a God allow the unrighteous to go on forever "destroying nations without mercy" (Habakkuk 1:17)? God assures Habakkuk that the wicked will be punished and "the righteous person will live by his faithfulness" (2:4).

Habakkuk 2:5-20. At some points in this series of woes, the prophet appears to address a sinful and treacherous nation, such as Assyria or Babylonia. At other points, he seems to speak to evildoers among his own people. In the present context, those addressed probably are the Assyrians. However, the indictments could be applied to individuals as well as nations.

Habakkuk 3:1-19. What is identified as a "prayer" is in fact a hymn or song of praise. Old Testament hymns are prayers in the sense that they are addressed to God. The hymn celebrates the appearance of God to intervene against the nations and thus bring salvation to the people. The God who now acts in wrath against the wicked is the one before whom all creation trembles.

DIMENSION THREE: WHAT DOES THE BIBLE MEAN TO ME?

The Vengeance of the Lord

You might approach the discussion of this uncomfortable theme in four steps. The first step is to acknowledge that it presents a problem for us. We need to admit to one another how such a point of view makes us uncomfortable. What are the roots of that discomfort, that temptation to lay aside such books as Nahum and Habakkuk? Such feelings probably stem from the fact that we have taken seriously the teachings of Jesus to love our enemies (Luke 6:27-28; Matthew 5:44). Many have been tempted to see the God of the New Testament as a God of love and the God of the Old Testament as a God of vengeance. But the New Testament writers see God, the Father of Jesus Christ, as the same God at work in the history of Israel.

The second step is to allow Nahum and Habakkuk to have their say. We need to hear and understand what they said. The books are, after all, part of our Bible. If we are to learn from and have our lives shaped by the Bible, then we cannot restrict ourselves to those books and passages that we already know and appreciate. Once we place Nahum and Habakkuk into their historical context, several points become clear. The most important is that the cry for vengeance comes from a people who have suffered from Assyrian imperialism and aggression. That cry is the voice of those who have been oppressed for centuries by the great world powers. Furthermore, their words are not simply political and nationalistic, but theological and moral. They are theological in that they view the world struggle as a conflict between God and the gods of the nations, especially Assyria (Habakkuk 2:18-20). So for Nahum and Habakkuk, the defeat of Assyria is a vindication of the power of God. The cry for vengeance is morally informed. The cry is based on a certain understanding of justice; that God will, within history, even the scales. The righteous will be vindicated, and the unrighteous will get what they deserve.

Once we have allowed Nahum and Habakkuk to have their say in their own historical situations, then the third step is to put their words into a wider biblical context and evaluate them. We do not even have to look to the New Testament to discover texts that present alternatives to the cry for vengeance. Earlier, we encountered the Book of Jonah, which seems to argue directly against the viewpoint in the Book of Nahum. Both books are about Nineveh. But the writer of the Book of Jonah ridicules the prophet who cannot find room in his heart to accept Nineveh's repentance or the Lord's forgiveness of Nineveh. In Micah 4:1-4, we have seen a vision of the kingdom of God that goes far beyond that in Nahum and Habakkuk. That vision is of a just world in which all nations live together in peace. In this prophet's vision, the weapons of war are made into tools to feed the hungry.

And then the New Testament includes the teachings of Jesus that we are to love our enemies. It seems likely that we will decide that Nahum and Habakkuk do not have the last word on the question of the relationship of the people of God to their enemies.

The fourth step, then, is to ask what message these books have for us in our time. Two points, in particular, are important. First, reading Nahum and Habakkuk as part of our Scriptures might help us hear and understand similar bitter cries for vengeance in our time. They are the voice of the marginalized and the vulnerable, the voice of those who have been powerless before terrible and terrifying enemies. People, individuals and nations, who have suffered from military invasion or other oppression, find it difficult to love those they consider their enemies. We need not agree that such views are right in order to understand them. Second, we might ask if Nahum and Habakkuk, whose attitudes we see as less than Christian, do in fact confront us with ourselves. That is, do we as American Christians also feel that it would be better if our enemies were destroyed? If we have that belief, how should we respond? How can we bring such viewpoints and impulses into the light of the Christian gospel?

You may wish to conclude the session by asking the members of the group to list what they have learned from their study of the books of Nahum and Habakkuk. Note the questions for further reflection raised by these two prophets.

Seek the LORD, all you humble of the land / . . . / perhaps you will be sheltered / on the day of the LORD's anger. (Zephaniah 2:3)

10

THE REIGN OF GOD

Zephaniah 1–3 and Haggai 1–2

DIMENSION ONE: WHAT DOES THE BIBLE SAY?

Answer these questions by reading Zephaniah 1

1. When did the word of the Lord come to Zephaniah? (1:1)

The word of the Lord came to Zephaniah in the reign of Josiah the son of Amon, king of Judah.

2. What does God say will be swept away? (1:1-2)

God says that everything will be swept away from the face of the earth, including people, animals, birds, fish, and idols.

3. Who does God promise to punish on the day of the Lord's sacrifice? (1:8-9)

God will punish the princes, the king's sons, those clad in foreign attire, and those who fill the temple of their gods with violence and deceit.

4. Who does the Lord promise to punish when searching out Jerusalem with lamps? (1:12)

God will punish "those who are complacent," who think that the Lord will do nothing either good or bad.

5. What kind of day is the day of the Lord? (1:15-16)

That day is a day of wrath, distress, anguish, trouble, ruin, darkness, gloom, and a day of trumpet and battle cry against the fortified cities and the corner towers.

Answer these questions by reading Zephaniah 2

6. What is the shameful nation called to do? (2:1)

    The shameless nation is called to gather together.

7. What are the humble of the land told to do? (2:3)

    The humble of the land are admonished to seek the Lord, to seek righteousness, and to seek humility.

8. What threat does the "woe" cry introduce? (2:5)

    The "woe" cry introduces a threat that the word of God is against Canaan, land of the Philistines, and the Lord will destroy it.

9. Why are Moab and the Ammonites being punished? (2:8-9)

    Moab and the Ammonites are being punished because of their insults against God's people and their threats against their land.

10. What does the prophet say will happen when God's hand is stretched out against the north? (2:13)

    Assyria will be destroyed and Nineveh made desolate, as dry as the desert.

Answer these questions by reading Zephaniah 3

11. How does the oppressing city that is rebellious and defiled behave? (3:1-2)

    That city obeys no one, accepts no correction, does not trust in the Lord, and does not draw near to God.

12. What are the officials, rulers, prophets, and priests of the oppressing city like? (3:3-4)

    The officials are roaring lions, and the rulers are "evening wolves" that leave nothing for the morning. The prophets are arrogant, treacherous people, and the priests profane the sanctuary and do violence to the law.

13. Which people does God promise to remove and to leave in the city? (3:11-12)

    God promises to remove "arrogant boasters," and leave "the meek and humble" within the city.

14. Why are the daughters of Zion and Jerusalem rejoicing? (3:14-15)

God has taken away their punishment and turned back their enemies; the Lord is with them.

Answer these questions by reading Haggai 1

15. When did the word of the Lord come to Haggai the prophet, and to whom was that word addressed? (1:1)

The word of the Lord came to Haggai on the first day of the sixth month of the second year of King Darius. It was addressed through Haggai to Zerubbabel, the governor of Judah, and to Joshua, the high priest.

16. What do the people say concerning the Lord's house? (1:2)

"The time has not yet come to rebuild the LORD's house."

17. What does God say through the prophet about the way the people have fared? (1:6)

They have planted much and harvested little; they eat and drink but do not have enough; they have clothes but are not warm. They have not fared well.

18. Why have the people expected much that turned out to be little? (1:9)

God "blew away" what they brought home because the Lord's house lies in ruins while they are busy with their own houses.

19. What did Zerubbabel, Joshua, and the people do? (1:12)

Zerubbabel and Joshua obeyed the voice of the Lord and the message of Haggai the prophet, and the people feared the Lord.

20. What happened on the twenty-fourth day of the sixth month? (1:14-15)

Zerubbabel the governor, Joshua the high priest, and the spirit of the whole remnant of the people came and worked on the house of the Lord.

Answer these questions by reading Haggai 2

21. What does the Lord promise to do concerning the present house? (2:9)

The Lord promises that the glory of the present house will be greater than that of the former one. "And in this place I will grant peace."

22. What is the first question God instructs Haggai to ask the priests? (2:11-12)
    God instructs Haggai to ask the priests whether consecrated meat carried in the fold of their garments makes what it touches consecrated.

23. What is Haggai's second question to the priests? (2:13)
    Haggai asks the priests if consecrated things become defiled if they are touched by someone who has become defiled because of contact with a dead body.

24. What does the Lord promise to do to Zerubbabel, and why? (2:23)
    The Lord promises to take Zerubbabel and make him like a signet ring, for God has chosen him.

DIMENSION TWO:
WHAT DOES THE BIBLE MEAN?

Background. This lesson takes up the study of two brief but important prophetic books, Zephaniah and Haggai. The books come from different eras in the history of Judah and address different problems. Consequently, the books are quite different in both form and content.

Introduction to Zephaniah. Zephaniah was active in the seventh century BC, not long before 621 BC. The book is a collection of prophetic speeches in four parts. The first part (1:2–2:3) announces judgment against Judah and Jerusalem. It includes the threat of the terrible day of the Lord. Trouble is coming, says the prophet, because of the pagan and idolatrous practices of the people and their leaders. The second part (2:4-15) is a series of woes against certain foreign nations. In the third section (3:1-13), the prophet returns to announcements of punishment against Jerusalem. These announcements include the message that the punishment will purify God's people and leave a remnant of those who seek the Lord. The final section of the book (3:14-20) contains announcements of salvation to Jerusalem and expressions of celebration that such salvation has come.

The first verse of the book places Zephaniah in the reign of the Judean king Josiah (640–609 BC). Other seventh-century prophets we have encountered are Nahum and Habakkuk. They were active near the time of the fall of the Assyrian city of Nineveh in 612 BC. Zephaniah could also have been a younger contemporary of Jeremiah.

During this time, Judah continued to live under the thumb of the Assyrian Empire. The kings who preceded Josiah, Manasseh (687–642 BC) and Amon (642–640), appear to have been virtual puppets of Assyria. According to the reports in Second Kings, they had allowed foreign religious practices to flourish in Judah. According to the Old Testament, the most important event in Judah during this era was a series of religious reforms begun by King Josiah. The events are reported in

2 Kings 22–23. The king ordered repairs to the Temple. While the repairs were in progress the high priest sent word to the king that he had found "the Book of the Law." When the book was read to Josiah, he saw that present religious practices fell far short of what the book required. He thus initiated a series of reforms. These reforms included the destruction of all places of worship other than the Temple in Jerusalem. He prohibited the worship of all foreign gods. The discovered book that provided the basis for the law was the central part of the Book of Deuteronomy.

Josiah's reform was not without its political implications and motivations. If the worship of foreign deities was to be prohibited, then among the first to go would be those of the Assyrians. Throwing the symbols of Assyrian religion out of Jerusalem would have been the same as rebellion against the Assyrian Empire. But by the time of the reforms, Assyrian power was already on the wane.

Zephaniah probably preceded this reformation, which took place in 621 BC. The book reflects no direct information concerning such events. It does attack the kind of religious mixture of legitimate and pagan practice also identified as problems by the reformers. In some ways, then, Zephaniah may have been a forerunner of Josiah's reform.

Zephaniah 1:1. Whether the Hezekiah from whom Zephaniah was descended was the king by that name cannot be known for sure. It seems quite likely that he was. Zephaniah certainly was from Jerusalem. He lived in the shadow of the Temple, and had dealings with the upper class. Also noteworthy in the genealogy of the prophet is the name *Cushi*. This name usually means "the Ethiopian" and refers to a black person from Africa.

Zephaniah 1:2–2:3. This section of the book presents a prophetic message of doom. The doom is so total that it is almost apocalyptic in nature. The central theme is the day of the Lord as a time when all sinners in the world will be punished. The beginning verses emphasize that the judgment is cosmic in scope. God will totally destroy everything and everyone on the face of the earth (1:2-3). Then attention is focused on Judah and Jerusalem (1:4-6). They will not escape God's wrath. Specifically threatened are those in Judah who have worshiped Baal, the idolatrous priests, the ones who worship the stars or the god Molek. In short, all who do not seek God must face the Lord's wrath. Next the prophet singles out the officials and even the sons of the king (1:7-9). Then Zephaniah describes the scene on the day of judgment. Cries and shouts will be heard. God will "search Jerusalem with lamps" to find and punish those who say that the Lord will do nothing (1:10-13). All this means that the day of the Lord is near (1:14- 18). Because human beings have sinned against God, they will suffer. Their wealth cannot save them from the end planned for them. But then, the prophet cries, there is hope for some. He calls for the "humble of the land, / you who do what he commands" to come together, to seek righteousness and humility (2:3). Possibly they may escape the wrath of the Lord, but both attitudes and actions must be changed.

Zephaniah 2:4-15. This section is a collection of prophecies against foreign nations. Pronouncements of such judgments by prophets must have been a regular part of some services of worship in Jerusalem. They would have served a purpose similar to praying for the defeat of enemies. As noted in the participant book, there appears to be a geographical order to the series. The prophet condemns nations at all four points of the compass. With the exception of the Cushites, who are noted only briefly (2:12), the reasons for the judgments are spelled out as arrogance, and especially arrogant behavior toward Judah. This section also contains a persistent note of condemnation against the religious practices of these enemies. This condemnation is consistent with the criticism of the worship of foreign gods by the inhabitants of Judah (1:4-9).

Zephaniah 3:1-13. The prophecies against the foreign nations are followed by a prophecy against Jerusalem. The speech begins with the same cry of "woe" that began the prophecies against the nations in chapter 2. Like most other prophecies of punishment, this one has two major parts. The first is the indictment, or the statement of the reasons for the punishment (3:1-7). The prophet begins with a general and comprehensive accusation. Those who live in the city listen to no one. They accept no correction, and do not trust in the Lord (vv. 1-2). Then the leaders in particular are indicted. They include the officials, rulers, prophets, and priests (vv. 3-5). The final reasons for punishment are that God brought trouble, hoping that the people would repent, but they were even more corrupt (vv. 6-7). The second part of the prophecy is the announcement of punishment (3:8-13). But the announcement here is different from most of those in earlier prophetic books. This announcement is of total judgment against all the nations, and of a punishment against Jerusalem. This punishment will cause the people to call upon the Lord. It will remove the proud and arrogant from Jerusalem. Only a humble and lowly remnant of those who seek the Lord will be left.

Zephaniah 3:14-20. The tone and content of these final verses are quite different from the rest of the book. Darkness has become light. Fear and terror have become hope and celebration. As the book now stands, the purpose of these lines is to spell out the good news that lies beyond the punishment. This section possibly was added in a later age, such as the time of the Babylonian Exile. It might have been added by those who had actually been through the fires of destruction and could now look to a time of celebration (v. 20).

Introduction to Haggai. The prophet Haggai was active about a century later than Zephaniah. All of the prophecies are dated quite precisely in the year 520 BC. The book, which does not have a title or superscription as such, contains four prophecies and one report of the response to a prophecy. In the first prophecy (1:1-11), the prophet instructs the people to rebuild the Temple. A report that the people have begun to do so follows (1:12-15). The second prophecy (2:1-9) promises that the glory of the new Temple will surpass that of the former one. The people will also prosper. In the third prophecy (2:10-19), the prophet explains that while ritual uncleanness is contagious, holiness is not. The fourth and final prophecy (2:20-23) announces that God has chosen Zerubbabel and will make him "like a signet ring."

Much happened to the people of God in the century between Zephaniah and Haggai. Assyria, which had threatened Judah and Israel for centuries, fell to the Babylonians in 612–609 BC. The generation after the reform of Josiah, in 621 BC, saw worship centralized in the Temple in Jerusalem. That very Temple had been destroyed by the Babylonians under Nebuchadnezzar. Jerusalem actually fell twice, in 597 and 587 BC. Both times, Judeans were carried off to exile in Babylon. Babylon fell in 538 BC to what would become the Persian Empire under Cyrus. The captives then were allowed to return and begin rebuilding Jerusalem. When Haggai began to address the people in Jerusalem, some eighteen years later, in 520 BC, the Temple had not yet been rebuilt.

Haggai was active during the time of the Persian Empire. This empire lasted for two centuries, from 538 BC until Alexander the Great conquered Darius III in 331 BC. The people of Judah thought of Persian rule as benevolent. Judah was a province of the empire. In the time of Haggai, Zerubbabel, a descendant of the Davidic dynasty, was the native-born governor. Freedom of religion was allowed. However, the situation for the people of God was quite different from what it had been before the Exile. Before, church and state had been one; the king governed on behalf of God. Now, state and religion were distinct. The people did not control their own political destiny, but religious institutions centered in the Temple flourished.

Haggai is a bridge between prophetic and priestly roles, institutions and ideas. He speaks the language of the prophets. He addresses the people with words from God, announcing the future acts of God, as the older prophets had. However, his messages concern the importance of building the Temple. The people will benefit if they do so. He also makes the distinction between sacred and profane things. Such words would be difficult to imagine from the mouth of Amos, Micah, or Hosea. Moreover, we look in vain among his words for the passionate concern for justice and righteousness that rings through the messages of the earlier prophets.

Haggai 1:1-11. The first divine revelation through Haggai tells the people to build the Temple. The people have obviously been able to rebuild their own houses and "paneled houses" (v. 4) for the governor and the high priest. But, though they have worked hard, they have not begun to prosper. Haggai relates this lack of success directly to the failure to work on the Temple. A drought, an act of God, confirms that view. The implication is that prosperity will follow if energy is given to building the Temple.

Haggai 1:12-15. Zerubbabel the governor, Joshua the high priest, and all the remnant of the people listened to the prophet and began work on the Temple. The reference to the people as "the remnant," recalls old prophetic words concerning those who would be left after God's judgment. The work described here probably was of the foundations being laid (see also Zechariah 4:9).

Haggai 2:1-9. Work on the Temple had hardly begun when problems arose. This prophecy is the response to those problems. Complaints have arisen because of disappointment with the new Temple, compared to the previous one. Haggai asks if anyone remembers the old Temple in its former glory. Few, if any, could possibly remember the first Temple, for it had been torn down sixty-seven years earlier. The comparison is probably between the present reality and the legend of Solomon's glorious Temple. But the problem, to judge by the prophet's response, was deeper than disappointment in the building. The Temple, like the kingship of the dynasty of David, symbolizes the kingdom of God. The people must have begun to doubt that the Lord was with them. They want the Lord to intervene to establish God's kingdom. Haggai assures them that God will indeed intervene, shaking the heavens. All the nations will then pay tribute to the Lord.

Haggai 2:10-19. The practice of asking priests about matters of worship must have been important in Israelite religious life. The law did not and could not cover all circumstances. So, when uncertainty arose, a layperson would ask the priests. The priests' answer would be an "instruction" or *torah*. In this instance, Haggai is told by God to ask whether something can become holy if it is touched by a sacred thing. The answer no would have been generally known. He then poses a second question. Does contact with a ritually defiled person render an object defiled? The answer is yes. Impurity can be communicated, but holiness cannot. Haggai then applies this principle to the present situation with the people (2:14). He concludes that the people are ritually defiled or unclean. Everything they offer to God is defiled. Certainly, he means that uncleanness has been spread throughout the community, but he does not identify its source. Some commentators have speculated that its source is the Samaritans among the people. However, impurity could stem from a great many factors, including contact with a dead body. The law provided rituals of purification. Possibly, the people had not been sufficiently scrupulous with such observances.

Haggai 2:20-23. In this final prophecy, Haggai reveals messianic expectations. He assures Zerubbabel, the descendant of the Davidic kings, that God has chosen him and will make him "like my signet ring" (2:23). Finding the promise of a Davidic ruler in a book otherwise focused upon the building of the Temple is not unusual. From the time of David himself (see 2 Samuel 7) and through such prophets as Isaiah, the establishment of the Temple on Mount Zion and the divine gift of the Davidic dynasty had been joined.

DIMENSION THREE: WHAT DOES THE BIBLE MEAN TO ME?

The Reign of God and Human Responsibility

In different ways, both prophets expect the Lord to intervene and establish God's kingdom. For Zephaniah, that intervention will be in the form of the day of the Lord. Some saw the day as one of victory for Israel over its foes. But, like Amos, Zephaniah announced that it would be a day of God's judgment against the chosen people as well, with violence and bloodshed. But that would not be the last word. The punishment would be purifying and cleansing. Only those faithful to God would be left in Jerusalem.

In a more subdued and less violent way, Haggai also expected God to establish a true kingdom. The Temple must be rebuilt. Haggai also hoped for re-establishment of the Davidic dynasty. For both, the kingdom was a time and place where God's will is done.

The people of God were involved in the inauguration of the kingdom. In Zephaniah, certain attitudes and actions would determine who lived in the time beyond the day of the Lord. To Haggai, human devotion, including building the Temple and attending to sacred matters, was necessary for God to act.

What kind of kingdom do we as Christians expect and hope for? Certainly, we look to a heavenly kingdom beyond death. The prophets did not have that kind of kingdom in view. They longed for a kingdom on this earth, within time. Does the Christian faith allow for such a hope, which can so easily become materialistic and even selfish? Each time we pray the Lord's Prayer, in what ways do we ask for such a reign of God in human history?

Certain qualities of life and certain behavior, according to these prophets, signal our part in God's kingdom. Those who are humble, devout, do God's will, and seek righteousness and justice are destined to participate. When such lives are lived, the kingdom of God may already be present in some measure.

But what of Haggai's promise that the people will prosper if they work on the Temple? Should we contribute to the construction of a church in order to become more prosperous in return? Not according to Haggai. In the name of God, Haggai calls the people away from concern with their own prosperity, wealth, and success. Fix your concern, he says, upon devotion to God. Demonstrate that devotion by building the Temple. God, who gives the earth and the rain, will see to your physical well-being.

Close the session by asking group members to list what they have learned about Zephaniah and Haggai. Write down on markerboard or a large sheet of paper the questions that have been raised.

The city streets will be filled with boys and girls playing there. (8:5)

11

VISIONS OF RESTORATION
Zechariah 1–8

DIMENSION ONE:
WHAT DOES THE BIBLE SAY?

Answer these questions by reading Zechariah 1

1. How is Zechariah identified? (1:1)

    Zechariah is identified as the son of Berekiah, son of Iddo, and as a prophet.

2. What does God tell Zechariah to say to the people? (1:3)

    The Lord tells Zechariah to tell the people that the Lord Almighty says, "Return to me . . . and I will return to you."

3. What does Zechariah say he saw in the night? (1:8)

    Zechariah says that in the night he saw a man mounted on a red horse, standing among trees in a ravine, and there were red, brown, and white horses in the background.

4. How did God answer the angel? (1:12-13)

    God spoke kind and comforting words to the angel.

5. What are the four horns? (1:18)

    In Zechariah's vision, the four horns are those who have scattered Judah, Israel, and Jerusalem.

Answer these questions by reading Zechariah 2

6. What is the man with the measuring line in his hand going to do? (2:2)

    The man is going to measure Jerusalem, to determine its width and its length.

7. What should those who are spread abroad as the four winds of heaven do? (2:6-7)

    They should flee from the land of the north and escape to Zion.

Answer these questions by reading Zechariah 3

8. Who is in Zechariah's vision? (3:1)

    In his vision, Joshua is standing before the angel of the Lord. Satan is also there in order to accuse him.

9. What does the angel say about the filthy clothes Joshua is wearing? (3:4)

    The filthy clothes must be removed from Joshua. Joshua's sin has been taken away, and he will be clothed with rich garments.

10. What does the angel of the Lord promise Joshua if he walks in God's ways? (3:7)

    Joshua will govern the Lord's house, have charge of the Lord's courts, and have "a place among these standing here."

11. What will happen when God engraves an inscription on the stone set up before Joshua? (3:9-10)

    God will remove the sin of the land in a single day, and in that day everyone will invite neighbors to sit under their vines and fig trees.

Answer these questions by reading Zechariah 4

12. To whom is the message concerning the lampstand, the bowl, and the olive trees addressed? (4:6)

    The message is addressed to Zerubbabel.

13. What is the word of the Lord concerning Zerubbabel? (4:8-9)

    Zerubbabel's "hands have laid the foundation of this temple" and they will also complete it.

14. How does the angel answer Zechariah's questions concerning the meaning of the two olive trees and the two branches of the olive tree? (4:11-14)

The two olive trees, as well as the two branches are the two anointed to serve the Lord of all the earth.

Answer these questions by reading Zechariah 5

15. What does Zechariah see when he looks again? (5:1-2)

Zechariah sees a flying scroll, thirty feet long and fifteen feet wide.

16. How is the meaning of the flying scroll explained to the prophet? (5:3-4)

The flying scroll is explained as the curse that goes out over the whole land. Anyone who steals or swears falsely will be banished.

17. What does the angel show Zechariah? (5:5-6)

The angel shows Zechariah a basket. The angel says that the basket is the iniquity of the people throughout the land.

18. What happened to the basket? (5:9-11)

The two women with wings like a stork took the basket to the land of Babylonia to build a house for it.

Answer these questions by reading Zechariah 6

19. How many chariots does Zechariah see, and what kind of mountains did they come out of? (6:1)

Zechariah sees four chariots, and they came from between mountains of bronze.

20. Where are the four chariots going? (6:5)

The chariots are the four spirits of heaven going out from the presence of God.

21. What does God tell Zechariah to do with the silver and gold? (6:9-11)

Zechariah is to make a crown, and set it on the head of Joshua, the high priest, the son of Jozadak.

Answer these questions by reading Zechariah 7

22. What is asked of the priests and the prophets? (7:2-3)

    The people ask if they should mourn and fast in the fifth month as they have done before.

23. What is the word of God that came to Zechariah? (7:8-10)

    The people are to administer true justice, show mercy and compassion, not oppress others, and not plot evil against each other.

24. Why would the Lord not hear when the people called? (7:13-14)

    The Lord would not hear because the people did not hear when God called to them.

Answer these questions by reading Zechariah 8

25. What does God promise to do for Zion and Jerusalem? (8:3)

    God will return to Zion and dwell in Jerusalem.

26. What are the people to do? (8:15-17)

    The people are to be truthful and sound in judgment, not plot evil against their neighbor, and not love to swear falsely.

27. In the days to come, what will ten people from all languages and nations do? (8:23)

    They will take hold of the robe of a Jew and say, "Let us go with you, because we have heard that God is with you."

DIMENSION TWO: WHAT DOES THE BIBLE MEAN?

Introduction to Zechariah. Zechariah was a contemporary of Haggai. Zechariah 1–8 contains three unequal parts. The first of these (1:1-6) is an introduction to the book, which takes the form of the prophet's call to the people to repent and return to God. The second and the major section (1:7–6:15) presents reports of Zechariah's eight night visions. In these vision reports, the prophet announces various aspects of the coming age of salvation for Judah. The Temple will be built. Anointed leaders will be designated. The will of God will be accomplished throughout the world. The third section (7:1–8:23) is a collection of various prophecies that begins and ends with messages concerning fasting.

The perspective and message of Zechariah are both prophetic and priestly. This prophet believes that he has received, in word and vision, God's message for the people. He shares with other priests concern for the Temple and its ritual. Above all, Zechariah is convinced that God is working to bring in a religious kingdom. This kingdom will have its center in Jerusalem.

Date and Circumstances. Like the oracles of Haggai, most of the speeches and vision reports in Zechariah 1–8 are dated according to the years of the Persian ruler Darius. All of them also give the month, and some even the day of the revelation. Since we know the dates of the Persian kings, we can date Zechariah's work to 520–518 BC. His first message came only two months after Haggai began his work. What was said in the previous lesson concerning the era of Haggai applies to Zechariah as well. Both prophets worked with and supported Joshua the high priest and Zerubbabel the governor. They especially worked to rebuild the Temple and establish a new religious life for the people as they returned from the Babylonian Exile. According to Ezra 6, the new Temple was dedicated in the sixth year of Darius, 515 BC.

More information about this critical era for the people of Judah can be found in the books of Ezra and Nehemiah. In addition to the basic problems of survival, the returning exiles and their fellow Judeans who had remained around Jerusalem must have faced a great many problems. Many would have mixed feelings about living under Persian rule, even though that rule was generally benevolent. For one thing, Jerusalem and the surrounding territory were part of an administrative district of Samaria. This arrangement stirred up ancient animosities. The people of God also believed the ancient promise (2 Samuel 7) that a descendant of David should always sit on the throne in Jerusalem. Some evidence, including the references in Zechariah 6:9-15 and Haggai 2:20-23, speak of an attempt to crown Zerubbabel the legitimate heir to David's throne. That act would have constituted revolution against the Persians. But increasingly, the hope for a royal messiah was applied to the life of religious practice. The people of Judea became a religion instead of a religious state. Zechariah played an important part in that transition.

The Night Visions. Eight distinct vision reports form the heart of these chapters. Keep in mind that these are reports. That is, we do not have direct access to the experiences. We must rely on what Zechariah tells us. And what he tells us is, after all, what was important to him. Each report conveys a message that he presents as a revelation from God.

The vision reports have important similarities. All of them are in the first person. Most of them begin with an introduction that alerts the hearer or reader that a report of a divine revelation is to follow. "Then I looked up" and "Then he showed me" are examples. The words for *seeing* in these introductions mean that special kind of seeing in a vision or dream. The next element is a description of the vision. The descriptions all include the interpretation of the meaning of what was seen. Generally, Zechariah hears the explanation from an angelic interpreter, whom he sees in the vision. In most cases, the visions include dialogue among the participants. Though he sometimes hears God speak, the prophet does not see the Lord directly.

The reader of these chapters is reminded immediately of the visions in the Book of Daniel. Both report dramatic sights. Their visions include angels, horns, the number four, and God's intervention to transform history for the sake of the people of God. Clearly, the two books are similar. But they have important differences as well. Zechariah's visions are not as bizarre or involved as Daniel's. The scope of divine transformation is not so comprehensive or violent in Zechariah. In fact, Zechariah is more like some of his prophetic predecessors, especially Ezekiel. The reports are even similar in important respects to those of Amos 7–9, from the eighth century BC. Zechariah's vision of a man with a measuring line in his hand (2:1) is strongly reminiscent of Amos 7:7. Like the vision reports of the other prophets, those of Zechariah concern a future that he sees taking place almost immediately. God is acting and will act within his lifetime.

Traditions and Theology. The contents and the speeches also take up traditions known in the earlier prophets. In fact, Zechariah makes a point of identifying himself as a prophet like those who have gone before (Zechariah 1:1-6). Like all the earlier prophets, he affirmed that the disaster of the Babylonian Exile happened because of the sins of the people. His theological thought runs back through Isaiah in particular. Both prophets, as well as their hearers, believed strongly that God had chosen Jerusalem, with Mount Zion as the most holy place. Moreover, Zechariah continues the concern with morality and social justice that characterized the earlier prophets. His message in 7:1-11 concerning behavior sounds almost like a catechism composed of the teachings of the preexilic prophets.

But Zechariah's words are different from earlier prophets in some important ways. He is concerned with priestly matters, such as the construction of the Temple, fasts, and ritual cleanness. His views and messages are similar in this respect to Ezekiel. In his time, the prophetic and priestly roles are similar, as the report in 7:3 suggests. Zechariah, who may have been from a priestly family, identifies himself quite closely with the priests. He connects the coming reign of God closely to the stones and mortar of the new Temple.

Zechariah 1:1-6. This speech alludes to the announcements of judgment by the early prophets. It reminds the hearers that what they said would happen did happen. Recollection of such matters becomes the text for a sermon by Zechariah, calling for repentance.

Zechariah 1:7-17. Like verse 1, verse 7 is a third-person report of the date of the revelation. It stands here as the heading to all eight night visions. The basic pattern of the vision and the meaning of its symbols are clear enough. Zechariah sees a man on a red horse standing in a ravine, with other horses behind him. They are the ones the Lord has sent out to patrol the earth. They will see that God's will is done. The message from the vision is an announcement of salvation to Judah. The exiles will come home, the Temple will be rebuilt, and the land will prosper. What is confusing is the identity of the figures in the vision. Various angels appear and speak, and a "man" is riding the red horse. This confusion may be the result of the editorial process. Or it may simply reflect the complexity of the prophet's impressions.

Zechariah 1:18-20. The horns symbolize the foreign powers that have brought trouble to the faithful. Horns generally refer to political power or force.

Zechariah 2:1-13. Verses 1-5 contain the third vision report. This report is followed in verses 6-13 by a prophetic speech. The meaning of the vision of a man with a measuring line is that Jerusalem and its walls will be rebuilt and inhabited. That God is to be "a wall of fire" around Jerusalem (v. 5) assures divine protection. The reference to God's "glory" within Jerusalem (v. 5) recalls one of the major traditions about the presence of God in the Temple. God does not literally live in the Temple, but God's glory will be there. For other expressions of this understanding see

Isaiah 6:3 and Ezekiel 1:28. Along with Ezekiel, Zechariah believed that God's presence left the Temple when the Babylonians took Jerusalem. The presence of God would return when the exiles came home and built it again. The prophetic speech in verses 6-13 is a call for the exiles to return and an announcement that such things will happen.

Zechariah 3:1-10. The point of the fourth vision is clear. Joshua, the high priest, is to be purified and crowned as head of the Temple. The age of peace will begin. Satan also appears in the vision "to accuse" Joshua. Instead, Satan is rebuked. Actually, *Satan* here is not a proper name but a title. The Hebrew should be read "the satan." In the Old Testament, the satan is an adversary or accuser, as in court. He is one who poses evil possibilities. Satan has no genuine power against God. Rather, he seems to occupy a status comparable to that of the angels who appear in Zechariah's visions. We are not informed of the content of his accusation against Joshua. In view of what follows, however, the accusation probably concerns ritual uncleanness.

Zechariah 4:1-14. While the fourth vision concerned the high priest, the fifth one focuses primarily on the governor Zerubbabel. He is to rule, but not as a conventional king. At the end of the interpretation of the vision, it becomes clear that there are two anointed ones, the high priest and the governor. With this text, we see some of the diverse messianic expectations in Judaism in the time of Jesus. Some looked for a ruler who was a military hero. Others looked for a suffering servant. Others came to expect the fulfillment of Zechariah 4:14: two messiahs, one priestly and one royal.

Zechariah 5:1-4. The size of the flying scroll indicates more than just its huge size. It would be about thirty by fifteen feet. The dimensions correspond to those of the portico of the Temple of Solomon (1 Kings 6:3). Scrolls with words of judgment are mentioned also in Jeremiah 36:2 and Ezekiel 2:9-10; 3:1-3. In those cases, as here, they indicate that the word of God has the power to effect judgment. Zechariah's scroll does not contain the names of the sinners, but the curse that will consume them.

Zechariah 5:5-11. At one level, the meaning of the seventh vision is obvious. "Wickedness" will be carried off to Babylon. But what kind of wickedness is not said. Two explanations are possible. Perhaps the female figure inside the container represents idolatry. It is only fitting that idolatry will be taken away from Jerusalem and to Babylon, the home of idols. If the wickedness is simply evil and its results—suffering—then the vision is a message of punishment directed against Babylon.

Zechariah 6:1-15. The final vision (vv. 1-8) is parallel in some ways to the first. Both contain horses of different colors, and they patrol the earth. The four chariots are to go to all the earth. (Only three are actually commissioned. None is sent to the east.) The emphasis is on the north country, that is, Babylon. God's sovereignty over the earth begins with those who have held God's people captive.

Zechariah 7:1-7. The date, 518 BC, introduces the series of prophetic speeches in chapters 7–8. In this first speech, Zechariah responds to a formal inquiry by two men from Bethel concerning a fast. He does not answer directly. He speaks about the purpose and meaning of fasts. He criticizes the people for thinking of their own satisfaction. The theme is resumed in 8:18-23. The intervening sections may have been inserted into the original message.

Zechariah 7:8-14. As in 1:1-6, the prophet bases a sermon on the message of the prophets before the Exile. The list of duties expresses the highest expectations for human behavior toward neighbors. Because their predecessors failed to follow such teachings, they went into exile. Zechariah identifies the prophets' teachings with the law. The law was the responsibility of the priests.

Zechariah 8:1-8. These lines convey a vision of Jerusalem at peace. Old men and women sit outside. The streets are full of children playing. The heart of the announcement is given in verse 8. The covenant between God and people will be renewed.

Zechariah 8:9-17. This speech is very similar to the message of Haggai. It calls for the Temple to be rebuilt and promises prosperity if the people respond. The remnant, those left over after the Exile, will be a blessing, just as they "have been a curse among the nations" (v. 13). The reference to the people as a blessing among the nations recalls the promise to Abraham (Genesis 12:1-3). Through Abraham and his descendants all the nations of the earth will be blessed.

Zechariah 8:18-23. These concluding verses proclaim joy and salvation for Jerusalem and the world. All fasts shall become occasions for celebration. Peoples from all over the world will come to the city of Jerusalem to pray to God. The foundation for such a hope had been expressed earlier in such texts as Isaiah 2:1-4 and Micah 4:1-4. Here, the faith of the Old Testament is carried out to its logical conclusion. If there is but one God, who has elected a people and a center for worship in Jerusalem, then the worship of that God is for all peoples. In Zechariah's time, there were those who would have disagreed with such a view, taking election as exclusiveness. But such passages as this one, along with the Book of Jonah, helped to pave the way for Jewish missionary activity in the time of Jesus.

DIMENSION THREE:
WHAT DOES THE BIBLE MEAN TO ME?

Church and State

The Old Testament struggles frequently with the proper form of government for the people of God. In the accounts of the rise of the monarchy in the time of Samuel and Saul, the people asked for a king. They wanted to be like all the other peoples of the earth. Some, including Samuel, reminded them that God was their king. But the issue was resolved in favor of a monarchy. As long as the people of God are in this world, some form of civil government is necessary. Later, those in Judah came to believe strongly that it was God's promise that a king (an anointed one) in the line of David would always sit on the throne. During the monarchy, church and state were one.

The exiles returning from Babylon knew that a return to the old way was not possible. The nation no longer existed. The people lived in Judea as part of one district of one province of the Persian Empire. To be sure, hope for national independence and the unification of civil and religious government never died.

Zechariah knows the old traditions of the anointed one, but he envisions a very different kingdom. The center of life will be in the Temple, religious practices, and faithful behavior. What had been the nations of ancient Israel and Judah is becoming Judaism, a religion.

The separation of church and state is one of the principles of American democracy. But how should church and state relate to each other? Surely, the form of government, the policies and actions of government, are not matters of indifference to Christians, either as individuals or as organized churches. Ask the group: What are some appropriate and effective ways for Christians to see that their convictions have some bearing on governmental policies and actions? Churches and religious groups are often seen as special interest groups like many others in the society. Ask the group to consider whether church and state should be more or less directly related to each other than they are presently.

You may wish to conclude the session by asking the members of the group to list what they have learned from their study of Zechariah 1–8.

Rejoice greatly, Daughter Zion! / Shout, Daughter Jerusalem! (9:9)

12

GOD'S FINAL VICTORY

Zechariah 9–14

DIMENSION ONE:
WHAT DOES THE BIBLE SAY?

Answer these questions by reading Zechariah 9

1. What will God do to Tyre? (9:3-4)

> *God will take Tyre's possessions, destroy its power on the sea, and consume Tyre by fire.*

2. How does Zion's king come to the city of Jerusalem? (9:9)

> *Zion's king arrives "righteous and victorious, / lowly and riding on a donkey.*

3. How extensive will be the king of Zion's dominion? (9:10)

> *His rule will extend from sea to sea, from the Euphrates River to the ends of the earth.*

Answer these questions by reading Zechariah 10

4. Why do the people wander like sheep? (10:2)

> *The people have no shepherd to guide them.*

5. At whom is God angry? (10:3)

> *God is angry at the shepherds, and will punish the leaders.*

6. When God signals for the people and brings them in, how many will there be? (10:8)

> *The people will be as numerous as before.*

7. What will happen to Assyria and Egypt? (10:11)

God promises that Assyria will pass through the sea of trouble and the scepter of Egypt will pass away.

Answer these questions by reading Zechariah 11

8. Why are the oaks of Bashan commanded to wail? (11:2)

The oaks of Bashan are commanded to wail because the dense forest has been cut down.

9. What do those who sell the flock say? (11:5)

Those who sell the flock say, "Praise the LORD, I am rich!"

10. What did the shepherd of the flock marked for slaughter name the two staffs? (11:7)

The shepherd named one staff Favor and the other Union.

11. What does the shepherd do to the staff called Favor? (11:10)

The shepherd he broke the staff, revoking the covenant with all the nations.

12. How much was God paid as wages by the sellers of the sheep? (11:12)

The sellers of the sheep paid God thirty pieces of silver.

13. What did it mean that the second staff, Union, was broken? (11:14)

The breaking of the second staff signified that the family bond between Judah and Israel was broken.

Answer these questions by reading Zechariah 12

14. What does God say Jerusalem will soon become? (12:2-3)

Jerusalem will become "a cup that sends all the surrounding peoples reeling" and "an immovable rock for all the nations."

15. What will the clans of Judah be like on that day? (12:6)

The clans of Judah will be "like a firepot in a woodpile, like a flaming torch among sheaves."

16. With whom will the feeblest of the inhabitants be compared on that day? (12:8)

On that day the feeblest of the inhabitants will be like David.

17. What does the Lord promise to pour out on the house of David and the inhabitants of Jerusalem? (12:10)

The Lord promises to pour out a spirit of grace and supplication on the house of David and the inhabitants of Jerusalem.

Answer these questions by reading Zechariah 13

18. Why will the fountain be opened? (13:1)

The fountain will be opened to cleanse Jerusalem from sin and impurity.

19. What will God banish from the land? (13:2)

God will banish the names of the idols from the land, and remove from the land the prophets and the spirit of impurity.

20. What will happen to the one-third left alive in the land? (13:8-9)

God will put the one-third left alive into the fire, refine them like silver, and test them like gold.

Answer these questions by reading Zechariah 14

21. What is to happen to the people when the nations gather against Jerusalem for battle? (14:2)

Half of the city will be taken into exile, and the rest will not be taken from the city.

22. What will flow out of Jerusalem? (14:8)

"On that day living water will flow out from Jerusalem, half of it east to the Dead Sea and half of it west to the Mediterranean Sea, in summer and in winter."

23. What will happen to the peoples that fight against Jerusalem? (14:12)

God will strike the nations that fought against Jerusalem with a plague of rot.

24. What will the survivors among the nations do year after year? (14:16)
    They will go up to Jerusalem to worship the King, the Lord Almighty, and to celebrate the Festival of Tabernacles.

25. What is to be inscribed on the bells of the horses? (14:20)
    "HOLY TO THE LORD" is to be inscribed on the bells of the horses.

DIMENSION TWO: WHAT DOES THE BIBLE MEAN?

Background. Chapters 9–14 contain a collection of somewhat diverse prophetic speeches. It is unlikely that they are the work of a single author or speaker. Long before the rise of biblical scholarship, some in the church believed that at least some of the speeches in these chapters were not written by the prophet responsible for Zechariah 1–8. The first Zechariah, Joshua the high priest, Zerubbabel the governor, or the problems of the construction of the Temple are not mentioned, for example. Considering other variations in style and point of view, it seems unlikely that Zechariah 9–14 was written by a single person. For example, Matthew 27:9-10 cites Zechariah 11:12-13 and attributes it to Jeremiah. The difference between poetic speeches in chapters 9:1–11:3 and prose addresses in the remainder of the book are obvious. Moreover, there are new titles at both 9:1 and 12:1. Many recent scholars see at least two prophetic figures behind the book. That there were even more is likely. The work then is a collection of prophetic speeches from a group that was confident that God would intervene in a dramatic fashion to establish the kingdom.

The first Zechariah was active at the very beginning of the Persian period, around 520 BC. These addresses in the latter chapters of Zechariah, then, probably come from the last of the fourth and the beginning of the third centuries BC. Allusions are made to the Greeks (9:1-8, for example) who appeared in the Near East with the conquests of Alexander the Great in 334 BC, which would date to about 200 years later than the first eight chapters of Zechariah.

The Old Testament prophetic tradition emerges at the point of a major world crisis and transition again. Earlier Haggai and Zechariah were active as Babylon fell. The Persians came to power, and the exiles came home to Jerusalem to rebuild their community. Nahum had been active as Assyria fell to the Babylonians. Even earlier, Hosea and Amos had foreseen the fall of the Northern Kingdom as Assyria expanded its empire.

The writers of Zechariah 9–14 could not have known what momentous changes would occur following Alexander's conquests. The little Jewish community soon would find itself threatened by powerful cultural forces from the West. It would be torn apart by struggles for power among Alexander's successors. Eventually, the Jews would mount a successful revolt in the second century BC.

By the time of Jesus, Judaism had several distinct parties, including the Pharisees and the Sadducees. The internal conflicts reflected in Zechariah 9–14 give some indications that such differences had a long history. But few of the details can be known for sure. These chapters signal important theological developments that will emerge later as apocalyptic literature. The movement in such a direction did not influence all of the community; the priestly leadership of the Temple was in conflict with such a view.

The collection has two main parts (9–11; 12–14). Each is introduced by its own superscription. The first part begins with an announcement of judgment against other nations (9:1-8). At first, the appearance of the Greeks is welcomed. Zechariah 9:11-17 condemns them, though. God is acting in and through historical events. The second part (chs. 12–14) also announces that God is acting and will act. This part views that action as a more dramatic transformation. The speeches in this section are distinctly more apocalyptic in nature. They are like the visions in the books of Daniel and Revelation. Both sections of the book reflect internal conflict and even controversy within the Jewish religious community.

Some of the uses of Scripture in Zechariah should be noted. Zechariah 9:1-6, for example, picks up some of the phrases in the series of announcements against foreign nations in Amos 1–2. Zechariah 12:1, "The LORD, who stretches out the heavens, who lays the foundation of the earth, and who forms the human spirit" seems to depend upon Isaiah 42:5. Zechariah 13:5, part of the criticism of prophets, quotes the response of Amos to Amaziah (Amos 7:14); Zechariah 14:5 refers to the same earthquake mentioned in Amos 1:1. The covenant formulas in Zechariah 13:9 pick up on an old tradition, as expressed especially in Hosea 2:21-23. Moreover, throughout these prophecies, there is confidence in the old traditions that see Jerusalem, with the Temple on Mount Zion, as the Lord's chosen place. God's promise to guard the Temple (9:8) continues a theme that had been present in Isaiah of Jerusalem in the eighth century BC.

The distinctive parts of these chapters concern the nature and extent of the coming kingdom of God. These chapters move us beyond the traditional prophetic expectation that God will intervene to judge and save. In Zechariah, we move in the direction of an apocalyptic vision. This view is even more pronounced in chapters 12–14 than in 9–11. In apocalyptic literature, such as Daniel and Revelation, God's intervention would utterly transform both history and nature. Zechariah 9–14 envisions a comprehensive transformation, including all peoples. But these chapters do not yet expect "a new heaven and a new earth" (Revelation 21:1). Jerusalem will be central, but it will not be the "new Jerusalem" of Revelation 21:2.

Very important seeds are planted here concerning the coming messiah. The tradition of a messiah in the line of David is maintained, but a new note is sounded. The one who is to rule will do so, not through military and political power, but through humility (Zechariah 9:9-10). Nonetheless, his reign will be from sea to sea. There can be no doubt that such hopes helped to prepare the way for an understanding of and faith in Jesus as the long-expected Messiah.

Zechariah 9:1-8. The heading, "A prophecy," is also found in Zechariah 12:1. The Hebrew word can also be translated "burden." Frequently in prophetic literature, this word introduces an announcement of judgment against foreign nations. The words of judgment are in the form of military disaster. The judgments are directed against some of Judah's near neighbors, by way of the country's main cities-- Syria (Hadrak, Damascus, and Hamath), Phoenicia (Tyre and Sidon), and four of the Philistine cities (Ashkelon, Gaza, Ekron, and Ashdod). The historical background of this prophecy seems to be the successful campaign of Alexander the Great into the area following his conquest of the Persian King Darius III. Darius was defeated at Issus in 333 BC.

The sequence of the cities and states in the announcement seems to correspond to the progress of Alexander's army. Those events marked the end of the Persian Empire and the beginning of the Hellenistic period in the Near East. The Hellenistic period lasted until 63 BC, when the Romans came under Pompey. Like other prophets before him, the writer of these lines sees a human king and his army as instruments of God's will.

An interesting and unusual note is sounded in verses 6-7. In the process of the destruction, Ashdod, "the pride of the Philistines," is to be transformed from a bloodthirsty people to "those who belong to our God." The reference to blood probably is an allusion to dietary practices. The law prohibited Jews from eating meat with the blood. The passage concludes with a strong note of reassurance to those who must have wondered if Judah and Jerusalem could expect trouble from this new front.

Zechariah 9:9-10. The Hebrew expressions for "Daughter Zion" and "Daughter Jerusalem" personify the cities as young women; *daughter* could also be "maiden." That hope for Jerusalem and Zion is connected with the expectation of a new king is not unusual. But what is utterly remarkable is that this king is meek and humble. He is one who does not rule by force but puts an end to the instruments of war. Whether or not the writer had a particular ruler in mind is not known. A people humbled by world events, as the Jews had been, could appreciate a humble messiah. As the account of the entrance of Jesus in to Jerusalem makes clear (Matthew 21:5; John 12:15), the earliest Christians saw the coming of Jesus as the fulfillment of this prophecy.

Zechariah 9:11-17. Three separate prophecies continue the good news. The first (vv. 11-13) announces that God will set the captives free, and then defeat the Greeks. This statement contrasts with the first part of the chapter where the march of the Greeks into the Near East is cause for celebration. The second prophecy (vv. 14-15) develops the ancient theme of the Lord as the Divine Warrior (see Exodus 15:1-3). Finally, the day of the Lord's salvation for "his flock" is described in glowing terms (vv. 16-17).

Zechariah 10:1-2. These verses are a prophetic instruction to the people concerning prayer. In the tradition of Hosea, the prophet insists that the people direct their prayers and inquiries only to God. Trusting in false gods' misleading diviners and the like leads only to trouble.

Zechariah 10:3-12. Several prophetic speeches have been assembled here. The first (vv. 3-5) announces that God will act against the shepherds of the flock. But the flock itself will be victorious over its enemies, because God is with them. The next speech (vv. 6-7) is an announcement of salvation for both the former Northern Kingdom (Joseph, Ephraim) and Southern Kingdom (Judah). The third unit (vv. 8-12) is another announcement of salvation. The dispersed peoples will be brought home from both Egypt and Assyria, and their enemies laid low. The return will be like another exodus from Egypt. Assyria and Egypt here probably stand for the Greek powers, the Ptolemies in Egypt and the Seleucids in Syria.

Zechariah 11:1-3. In this taunt song, the world powers are personified as mighty trees or animals.

Zechariah 11:4-17. The tradition of symbolic actions by prophets and the reports of such activities form the background of this speech. Prophets, such as Hosea and Isaiah, gave their children names that conveyed the particular message they had for their people from God. Isaiah 20 reports that, as a sign-act, Isaiah even walked about the city of Jerusalem naked and barefoot for three years. During the siege of Jerusalem by the Babylonians, Jeremiah bought a field from his cousin. This purchase was a sign that one day in the future, fields and houses would once again be bought and sold. Jeremiah had also walked around in Jerusalem wearing a yoke, saying that the people would be put under the yoke of Babylon. The basic elements of such reports, including these in Zechariah, are the account of the action and its interpretation. That is, the point of the activity is not simply to attract attention. The point is to convey the prophetic message, which, since it came from God, was understood to be effective. Breaking the staffs called Favor and Union signaled the annulment of the covenant between God and Israel, and the division between Judah and Israel. In taking up the implements of a worthless shepherd, Zechariah announces that the land will suffer under a worthless leader. Thus this passage announces judgment.

The historical context probably was a conflict within the postexilic Jewish community. The bad shepherds probably represent leaders the prophet does not approve of. The annulled covenant between Judah and Israel (v. 14) probably is a reference to ruptured relations between the returned exiles in Judah and the people of Samaria.

Zechariah 12:1–13:6. While they are prophetic in style, these announcements are very similar in content and perspective to apocalyptic literature. Other examples of this kind of apocalyptic literature are Daniel 7–12 and Revelation. The prophetic theme of the day of the Lord is employed. But this theme has changed from the time of the earlier prophets, like Amos. They expected divine intervention in the immediate future, and with a limited scope. This passage thinks in terms of a cosmic event and a final day of judgment. The writer and his audience see themselves living in the last difficult and trying days before God's victory. Jerusalem plays a key role in the drama of the last days. When enemies come up against it, they will be destroyed. The Davidic dynasty will be raised up again (12:7-8). Furthermore, there will come a time when the house of David and the people of Jerusalem will be given a spirit of compassion and supplication. They will mourn for "the one they have pierced" (12:10). John 19:34-37 takes these lines as a prophecy of the death of Jesus.

One aspect of the last days will be God's removal of the names of the idols, the prophets, and the impure spirit from the land (13:1). It seems strange to see prophets listed here with obviously corrupt religious practices. Strong condemnation of prophetic activity is even stranger. But there had always been conflicts between various prophets; Amos seems to have rejected the title (see Amos 7:14). This passage (Zechariah 13:5) alludes to those earlier words of Amos. It may be that our present passage has in view false prophets. The rejection seems to be sweeping, though. Perhaps it reflects a view in the postexilic religious community that the time of prophetic inspiration had come to an end.

Zechariah 13:7-9. The final judgment will sweep away the shepherd and destroy two thirds of the flock. The shepherd is probably some unidentified leader or high priest. The flock is the people. The one third who are saved will not necessarily be those who are especially righteous. The fires of the terrible day will purify and refine them into the people of God.

Zechariah 14:1-5. This announcement of the final day of battle is similar to the one in Zechariah 12. This announcement is more eschatological in tone and content. When God fights in Jerusalem against the enemies, the Mount of Olives will be split, and the entire terrain changed.

Zechariah 14:6-21. Even further dramatic changes in nature are in store. There will be continuous day, living waters will flow out of Jerusalem, and the entire land will be a plain. Thus, the Holy City will be elevated and seen by all. Those who oppose Jerusalem shall be destroyed by a plague. The language is highly symbolic. After the day of God's battle against the nations, those who survive will come up to Jerusalem to worship the one true king. The survivors will even participate in the Jewish festivals. Finally, ordinary pottery will become sacred, sufficient for the preparation of sacrifices. Given the great importance of ritual purity and the attitudes of exclusivism in the period, this final paragraph is a highly significant affirmation that goes far beyond such narrow attitudes.

DIMENSION THREE: WHAT DOES THE BIBLE MEAN TO ME?

The New Testament Meaning of the Old Testament

Many issues are raised in Zechariah 9–14 for contemporary Christians. Like most prophetic literature, and all apocalyptic expectations, these chapters confront us with the question of God's final purposes in history. Other matters that occupied the writers of these lines and that will also be of concern to us are the relationship of the chosen people of God to others and the qualities of those who lead or shepherd the community. However, one particularly significant issue raised by this lesson concerns the use of Old Testament texts in the New Testament.

Studying these chapters has revealed some of the more obvious Old Testament passages that are cited in the New Testament. You may begin this discussion by asking group members to begin adding to that list other texts in Zechariah 9–14 that have been given a New Testament or Christian meaning. Have someone list some of the other more important Old Testament passages that have been given new meaning by Christians and New Testament writers. These would certainly include Isaiah 9; 11; 42:1-9; 52:13–53:12; and Psalms such as 2; 45; 110.

A second step might be to review the meaning of such passages in their ancient Israelite context. The prophetic lines in Zechariah concerned persons, whom we may or may not be able to identify, and events in the postexilic Jewish community. Some of the Isaiah and Psalms passages concerned kings, actual or expected, in the dynasty of David. Perhaps the most important point to keep in mind is that *messiah* means "anointed one." The word originally referred to the king. In later times and in apocalyptic literature, it came to refer to the one who would be sent from God to participate in the establishment of God's reign.

The third step would be to reflect upon the New Testament meaning of such passages. Almost without exception, the earliest Christians saw that the coming of Jesus had fulfilled ancient prophecies of a messiah sent from God. But they were selective; in the time of Jesus, there were many different messianic expectations, including hopes for a military leader who would free the

Jews from Roman domination. The early Christians saw one in the line of David, a humble, but fully human messiah who, at the same time, was the Son of God.

A fourth step might be to face the issue of the difference between the Old and the New Testament meanings of these passages. It may seem obvious to many Christians that the New Testament meaning is preferred. We need to remind ourselves that the situation was the reverse in New Testament times. That is, the earliest Christians took for granted the truth and authority of what we now call the Old Testament. It was the new revelation that sometimes argued the case by citing the Jewish Scriptures.

All written materials, and especially important religious texts, take on a life of their own beyond the meaning and intentions of the original writers. The writers of Zechariah and Isaiah and Psalms did not have Jesus in mind. But later, once he had come, we see new and even deeper meanings in their words. This is the purpose of history. We can see that a suffering, redeeming messiah had been expected long before Jesus came.

We may be able to read such powerful Old Testament passages with two ears. One ear listens for the concrete and specific meanings of the words in their own times. For Christians, the other ear hears how such words help interpret for us the coming of Jesus. Our understanding of both the Bible and the Incarnation may thus be deepened.

You may wish to close the session by asking members of the group to list some of the things they have learned from their study of Zechariah 9–14. List these insights on a markerboard or a large sheet of paper if time allows.

I will send my messenger, who will prepare the way before me. (3:1)

THE MESSENGER OF THE LORD

Malachi 1–4

DIMENSION ONE: WHAT DOES THE BIBLE SAY?

Answer these questions by reading Malachi 1

1. What does God tell Israel? (1:2)

God tells Israel, "I have loved you."

2. What will God do if the people of Edom say they will rebuild their ruins? (1:4)

If the people of Edom build, God will demolish; they will be called the Wicked Land.

3. What does God ask the priests? (1:6)

God asks the priests, "If I am a master, where is the respect due me?"

4. What does the passage say about God's name? (1:11)

God's name is great among the nations, from the rising of the sun to its setting.

5. What do priests bring to the altar? (1:13)

The priests bring offerings that are injured, crippled, or diseased.

6. What does the Lord curse? (1:14)

The Lord curses the cheat who has an acceptable male in his flock, vows to give it, and then sacrifices a blemished animal instead.

Answer these questions by reading Malachi 2

7. For whom is the Lord's command? (2:1)

The Lord's command is for the priests.

8. What will happen if the priests do not honor God's name? (2:2)

If the priests do not honor the Lord's name, God will send the curse upon them and curse their blessings.

9. With whom did God make a covenant of life and peace? (2:4-5)

God made a covenant of life and peace with Levi.

10. What should the priests do? (2:7)

As messengers of God, the priests should preserve knowledge, so that the people may seek instruction from them.

11. How has Judah committed a detestable thing in Israel and Jerusalem? (2:11)

Judah has committed a detestable thing by desecrating the sanctuary of the Lord and marrying "women who worship a foreign god."

12. What has the one God done? (2:15)

The one God has made the people, body and spirit. God seeks godly offspring.

13. How have the people wearied God with their words? (2:17)

They say that everyone who does evil is good in the eyes of the Lord, and ask "Where is the God of justice?"

Answer these questions by reading Malachi 3

14. Who is God sending, and why? (3:1)

God is sending a messenger of the covenant to prepare the way before the Lord.

15. What is the messenger to do? (3:3)

    The messenger is to "sit as a refiner and purifier of silver," purifying and refining the Levites until they bring offerings in righteousness.

16. What does God promise to do if the people return? (3:7)

    God will return to the people, if they will return to God.

17. How are the people robbing God? (3:8)

    The people are robbing God in their tithes and offerings.

18. What does God tell the people to do, and why? (3:10)

    God tells the people to bring the whole tithe into the storehouse, so that there may be food in God's house.

19. What will happen when the Lord blesses the people? (3:12)

    When the Lord blesses the people, all nations will call them blessed, for they will be a delightful land.

20. How have the people spoken against the Lord? (3:13-15)

    The people say it is futile to serve God. They ask what they gain by carrying out God's requirements or going about like mourners. They consider the arrogant blessed and claim that evildoers not only prosper but also escape when they challenge the Lord.

21. What was written when those who feared God talked with one another and God heard them? (3:16)

    A scroll of remembrance was written of those who feared God and honored God's name.

Answer these questions by reading Malachi 4

22. What will happen to all the arrogant and all evildoers? (4:1)

    All the arrogant and all evildoers will be stubble. The Lord will burn them up, leaving them neither root nor branch.

23. What will be the fate of those who revere the name of the Lord? (4:2-3)

    Those who revere the name of the Lord shall leap like well-fed calves, trampling down the wicked.

24. What are the people told to remember? (4:4)

    The people are told to remember the law of God's servant Moses, the decrees and laws that God gave him at Horeb for all Israel.

25. What will Elijah do before the great and dreadful day comes? (4:6)

    Elijah will come before the great and dreadful day, and he will turn the hearts of the parents to their children and the hearts of children to their parents.

DIMENSION TWO: WHAT DOES THE BIBLE MEAN?

Introduction to Malachi. The Book of Malachi is an anonymous book. *Malachi* probably is not a proper name but the title *my messenger*, as indicated by Malachi 3:1. Stylistically, the words of this unnamed prophetic figure are unique. The book consists almost entirely of dialogues between God or the prophet and the addressees. This style lends a didactic and argumentative character to the work. The book consists of a collection of seven units. They are easy to distinguish from one another in terms of form and content.

Malachi 1:2-5, an address to the people concerning God's love for them, forms the first unit. Malachi 1:6–2:9 forms the second unit. This section is addressed to the priests and criticizes them for offering poor sacrifices. Section three, Malachi 2:10-16, addresses the Israelite men who abandon their wives to marry foreign women. Section four, Malachi 2:17–3:5, addresses those who doubt the justice of God. This section affirms that God will come to set things right.

Malachi 3:6-12, section five, is a disputation. It interprets the present distress of the people as caused by their failure to pay tithes and offerings. It promises that, if they will change, God will bless them. The sixth section, Malachi 3:13–4:3, is another argument with those who doubt the justice of God. These verses affirm that a day is coming when God will reward the faithful and punish evildoers. The seventh and final section contains the concluding verses, 4:4-5. These verses are not dialogue and dispute. They are an admonition to be faithful and a promise that Elijah will come before the day of the Lord.

The book gives us no direct information about the prophet, not even his name. The superscription does not include a date. The book contains no allusions to historical persons or groups by which we could establish a definite date for the prophet's work. Nevertheless, most scholars agree about the era from which the book comes. The evidence for dating the work includes the style and vocabulary, the theological perspective, and above all the assumptions about the religious life of the people addressed.

The book probably comes from the postexilic period, after the rebuilding of the Temple in 520 BC, and before the time of Ezra and Nehemiah (around 400 BC). The writer assumes that temple sacrifices have been offered for some time. This means that he arrived on the scene some time after Haggai and Zechariah, who are dated around 520 BC.

Likewise the prophet must be earlier than Ezra and Nehemiah, who came around 400 BC. This conclusion is based on the fact that Malachi addresses the kind of religious problems that Ezra and Nehemiah also faced. Ezra and Nehemiah are reported to have solved these problems. One problem concerned the proper legal ordering of the Temple cult. Malachi considers the order to be in a bad state. The other problem was the issue of intermarriage with foreigners. Moreover, the understanding of correct sacrifices does not take into account all the details of the law instituted by Ezra.

Thus the Book of Malachi comes from the heart of the Persian period, probably the middle of the fifth century BC. The allusion to a governor (1:8) would be to the one appointed by the Persian royal court. But apart from the concern with intermarriage, and negative thoughts about neighboring Edom (1:2-5), there is remarkably little interest in affairs outside of Judah. The territory of Israel, the ancient people of God, now consisted only of Judah, which was part of a province of the Persian Empire. The center of Judah was the city of Jerusalem. As far as we can tell, the people had to contend with few significant external threats. However, to judge from the Book of Malachi, their agricultural economy was far from prosperous.

As a rule, the Old Testament prophets give us remarkably little direct information about themselves. When they talk about their backgrounds or experiences, they do so in order to present the word of God, which is central. The Book of Malachi gives us no word about the prophet. His passionate concerns come through, however. There can be no doubt that he was a courageous individual, willing to take on any and all in the name of the Holy One of Israel.

A great many of the concerns are priestly and cultic. The emphasis on purity and proper sacrifice, and the concern with the law, show this interest. But at the same time, the message is prophetic. Like earlier prophets, this one presents the words of God to the people as a whole and to specific groups. He announces a threatening and promising future, and emphasizes the prophetic understanding of justice (3:5).

The word *prophet* may not be the best term for his role. He does speak in the name of God, and his words often concern the future that God has in store. But many of his concerns are more priestly than prophetic in the traditional sense. In fact, he seems to be identified with a particular priestly group, the Levites (2:4-9). In a subsequent age, clear conflicts developed in Jerusalem between priestly groups. The Levites lost out to the Zadokites. Possibly the writer of the Book of Malachi was a cultic prophet who identified with the Levitical priests.

Literature and Theology. The book has some of the typical features found in other prophetic books. One of these features is speeches in which the Lord is quoted directly. The book also includes some announcements concerning the future. But the most distinctive characteristic of the book is the form of the speeches as dialogues. Each speech is in the form of a disputation between God, or the prophet on God's behalf, and the group addressed. The words of the opponents are quoted, to indicate the problem to which the divine message responds.

The book, then, has an argumentative character. The arguments are a literary device used by the prophet, not accounts of actual conversations. The actual speaker throughout is the prophet, who says that the opponents say thus and so. The opponents are invariably presented in an unfavorable light. Some of the words placed in their mouths may be exaggerations of what they actually would have said. We do not know whether these discourses were, like those of earlier prophets, first delivered orally and then written down, or whether they originated as literary works.

The priestly aspects of Malachi's theology are the deep concerns for correct sacrifices and offerings. These represent for him the devotion and commitment called for in the ancient covenant. They express a concern for the holiness of the Temple, which must be maintained by proper ritual. The prophetic aspects of his thought are reflected in the concern for justice (3:5), and the expectation that God will intervene in history to establish the kingdom (3:1-5; 3:16–4:3). In this combination of priestly and prophetic interests, the Book of Malachi stands in the tradition of Ezekiel.

Malachi 1:1. The superscription used here is the same as the one in Zechariah 9:1 and 12:1. These three collections of prophetic addresses—Zechariah 9–11; 12–14; Malachi 1–4—appear to be the words of three anonymous prophets. As the Hebrew Bible was taking shape, the collections were placed at the end of the other small prophetic books. Malachi may have been set apart as a separate book and given a superscription in order to have twelve books.

Malachi 1:6–2:9. The speech begins with the citation of a proverb: "A son honors his father, and a slave his master." This saying, which states a generally accepted truth, becomes the foundation for God's questioning accusation. If that is normal behavior, then, says God, where is my honor as a father and my respect as a master? We can then recognize that God's quarrel is with the priests. They are accused of despising the Lord's name by offering polluted food on the altar. While the laity brought the sacrifices and offerings, the priests were responsible for interpreting and enforcing the laws of the offerings.

The accusation assumes certain ritual regulations for the animals of the sacrifice. Some of the laws concerning sacrifice are given in Deuteronomy 15:19-21, where the people are instructed to consecrate the firstborn of their herds and flocks to God. But if the animal has any blemish, if it is lame or blind, then it shall not be sacrificed. These laws in Deuteronomy seem to have in mind the sacrifice as a meal eaten "in the presence of the LORD" (Deuteronomy 15: 20) at the Temple in Jerusalem. Similar, but even more specific laws are found in Leviticus 22:17-25, which instructs that any sacrificial animal be without blemish.

The context of this passage is critical of those who do not give God proper reverence. Included in this context are some powerful hymnic phrases that affirm just how worthy of reverence God is. The Lord's name is great among all the nations, from the rising of the sun to its setting (1:11). The Lord is a king whose name "is to be feared among the nations" (1:14). To fear the Lord here, as in 1:6, is to stand in awe and reverence. The word *fear* is a synonym for proper worship.

The warning to the priests (2:1-9) contrasts those currently responsible for the Temple with the Levites. The priests are threatened with serious curses if they do not change their ways. They are reminded that God made a special covenant with the descendants of Levi, a "covenant of life and peace" (2:5). Levi, and presumably those who followed in his line, was faithful to his responsibilities. Those responsibilities included "true instruction," and turning people from sin (2:6). Priests, then, like prophets, are messengers of the Lord (2:7). Priests certainly should not show partiality in their instruction (2:9).

Malachi 2:10-16. This passage is a disputation addressed to Judean husbands. The passage is concerned with two closely related problems, intermarriage and divorce. The first matter is considered in 2:10-12. For a Judean to marry "women who worship a foreign god" (2:11) is an abomination. It is clear that the prophet understands the problem as a religious, rather than a national or ethnic, one. Perhaps he is concerned that such wives will lead their families away from worship of the Lord. Still, the perspective appears in contrast, if not conflict, with the assertion that opened the disputation: "Do we not all have one Father? Did not one God create us?" Apparently, when the prophet says "all," he means all Israelites.

The second part of the dialogue moves to the problem of divorce, as seen from the perspective of the divorced wives. The meaning of marriage as a covenant relationship is profoundly stated. The relationship should be one of loyalty between the two partners. At other points in the Old Testament, marriage seems to be understood more as a contract. The wife is viewed as the property of the husband. Divorce was not prohibited, but it was regulated, as Deuteronomy 24:1-4 indicates (see also Jeremiah 3:8; Hosea 2). Divorce seems to have been the sole prerogative of the husband; a woman could petition, but her husband would have to do the filing before their court. In Malachi 2:16, the statement that God hates divorce must be seen against that background. The statement affirms the sacredness of the relationship and concern for wives.

Malachi 2:17–3:5. Addressed in this disputation are those who have "wearied the LORD" with words, saying that God delights in those who do evil or that the God of justice is absent. These comments add up to the age-old question of the justice of God. This question is profoundly addressed in the Book of Job. Some among the faithful observe that it is not always the righteous who prosper (see 3:10-12). The prophet seems to have very little patience with the question. But the question is real, and is addressed in different ways elsewhere in the Bible. It becomes a particularly acute problem for those who believe that there is, or should be, direct and immediate retribution or reward based on obedience to divine law.

Here the message is that, while it may sometimes appear that God does not maintain justice, there will come a time when justice will be done. God will send a messenger to prepare the way. First, God will refine the Levitical priests so that proper offerings can be presented in Jerusalem. Then God will pronounce judgment against those who do not act in accordance with the law. The list of evildoers includes mainly those who oppress the weak (laborers, widows, orphans, and aliens), but also sorcerers, adulterers, and those who perjure. The God of Israel is a God of justice.

Malachi 3:6-12. This disputation is with the people. It accuses them of violating the ancient laws and calls for them to return to the Lord. The complaint that people rob God by failing to bring their offerings contrasts sharply with such earlier prophetic words as Amos 5:21-27 and Isaiah 1:10-17. Moreover, the message that God will bring immediate and material blessings on the people if they will bring offerings and tithes hardly seems to appeal to the highest motives. Matthew 6:25-34 puts the message quite differently.

Malachi 3:13–4:3. The issue of divine justice is taken up again in another dispute. This dispute is with those who assert that evildoers prosper. The prophet does not directly deny the allegation. He looks to a time in the future when God's justice will be established. The idea that a record book of some kind is being kept, to be opened in the last days, is also found in Daniel 7:10; 12:1; Revelation 20:12, and 21:27. If not in this time, then in the time to come, the righteous will be rewarded and the evil punished. It will be a glorious time for those who are faithful. The prophet probably has in mind a day within history and on this earth. This vision of the future is not as detailed or extensive as those in apocalyptic literature, such as Daniel and Revelation, but moves in that direction.

Malachi 4:4-6. Both of these little speeches probably were added by later editors and annotators. The first one (4:4) is a general admonition, similar to those in the Book of Deuteronomy, to obey the Mosaic Law. The other (4:5-6) picks up the theme of a messenger sent to prepare the way for the appearance of the Lord. The messenger is interpreted to be the prophet Elijah. Elijah became an increasingly important figure in the intertestamental literature and then in the New Testament. There, John the Baptist was seen as, in effect, a new Elijah preparing the way for the Lord.

DIMENSION THREE: WHAT DOES THE BIBLE MEAN TO ME?

Issues in Malachi

How are we to respond to the concern of the Book of Malachi with proper worship? The details of pure and proper sacrificial animals will be of little interest to modern Christians. But behind those details stands the still legitimate belief that what we give and bring to worship is of ultimate significance. Such gifts will indicate the seriousness and sincerity of our worship. Moreover, we might profit by wrestling with the question of the importance of sacred things and acts, such as our sacraments and our sanctuaries.

The second and third themes suggested in the participant book may be considered together. Does God directly reward those who are scrupulously faithful with sacrifices and offerings? What does it mean, then, that the righteous do not always seem to prosper?

Finally, how are Malachi's concerns for fair and just human relationships to be interpreted in our world? Why do the prophets seem so concerned to emphasize the responsibility of the people of God to care for the weak and powerless (Malachi 3:5)? The prophet's sayings on the meaning of marriage (Malachi 2:13-16) provide the foundation for some of our own reflections on the relationship of marriage to the divine will.

Several persistent themes are contained in the prophetic message. These themes are the power of the word of God to change history, the activity of God in history—in this world and not just beyond it—the prophets' emphasis on community and social institutions, their confidence in a just God who calls for justice and righteousness, and their firm conviction that God intends to establish the kingdom. The group members may feel the need to discuss any of these topics. This final lesson would be a good time to do so.

Ask the group members to conclude this lesson and the study of the Minor Prophets by listing and reflecting on any other important themes they have found.

CPSIA information can be obtained
at www.ICGtesting.com
Printed in the USA
FSHW011459080221
78302FS